THE LONELY VICTORY

Mt. Everest '78

PETER HABELER

translated from the German by DAVID HEALD

SIMON AND SCHUSTER • NEW YORK

1 2 3 4 5 6 7 8 9 10

Published in cooperation with Arlington Books, London

Library of Congress Cataloging in Publication Data

Habeler, Peter.
    The lonely victory.

    Translation of Der einsame Sieg.
    1. Habeler, Peter.   2. Mountaineers—Austria—
Biography.   3. Messner, Reinhold.   4. Everest, Mount—
Description.   I. Title.
GV199.92.H32A3413   796.5'22'0924 [B]   79-13741

ISBN 0-671-24842-1

Black and White Photos:
Peter Habeler, pages 10, 11, 14, 18, 20, 21, 22, 93, 109, 111,
113, 135, 148, 151, 154, 155.
Reinhold Karl, pages 37, 44, 83, 106, 141, 199.
Wolfgang Nairz, page 207.
Alfred Strobel, pages 213, 214.
Jürgen Winkler, pages 34, 35, 39, 41, 42, 43, 60, 61, 62, 63,
65, 70, 71, 73, 74, 75, 96, 163, 172, 174.
All color photos by Peter Habeler except the following:
Reinhold Messner, numbers 20, 21.
Jürgen Winkler, number 12.

For Regina

I

T HE VOICE of the Air India pilot roused me from restless semiconsciousness: "Ladies and gentlemen, welcome aboard our direct flight to New Delhi. We have now reached our cruising altitude of 29,000 feet; the temperature outside is about minus 22 degrees Fahrenheit."

A routine announcement for the pilot, but for me it contained a fascinating piece of information: 29,000 feet —that was, within a few feet, exactly the height of Mount Everest, the highest mountain in the world and the goal of our expedition.

If everything went well, in about six weeks' time I would be standing on the summit of that mountain, 29,028 feet, or 8848 meters, above sea level. Of its kind it would be a genuine first ascent, because twenty-five years ago on the twenty-ninth of May 1953 Edmund P. Hillary and his Nepalese companion, Tenzing Norgay, had outwitted the hitherto unconquerable mountain by means of a trick. They had, like all successful expeditions after them, used oxygen equipment. We, Reinhold Messner and myself, wanted to attempt the seemingly impossible—the first ascent of Mount Everest without artificial oxygen.

When, in the last two-and-a-half years, we had talked about our ambition—to climb Everest without the help of oxygen—hardly anyone had encouraged us. On the contrary almost everybody, whether they were mountaineers, altitude physiologists, or doctors, had strongly advised us against it. "It just can't be done; either you will never get to the top or you will never get down again, or if you are very lucky, you will get back as gibbering idiots. The lack of oxygen at this altitude kills the brain cells after only a few minutes and, what is more important, it destroys cells that are needed for the most important human functions. First of all your memory will be disturbed, then your speech center, and finally you will lose your sight and your hearing. Everest without oxygen is suicide."

Experiments in compression chambers had shown that at an altitude of about 26,000 feet the capacity for controlled thinking and action disappears. Within a short time you become unconscious; on a mountain you will meet certain death. All the great conquests of summits over 26,000 feet therefore, have only been achieved with the help of artificial oxygen; the Nānga Parbat, the K2, the Lhotse.

There was only one counterargument. As early as 1924 the Englishmen, Norton, Mallory and Irvine, attempted an assault on Everest despite their primitive equipment. Norton—the leader of the expedition—reached an altitude of 28,126 feet, apparently without suffering any damage to his health.

When we reminded people of this, they countered immediately with: "Yes, but what happened to Mallory and Irvine? They disappeared during the assault on the summit and nobody has ever seen them again. They were killed on Everest, whether they reached the summit before their death or not."

This was certainly true and since the 1920s nobody has even attempted to conquer the summit of Everest again without oxygen. Even with oxygen equipment, and using the most modern technology available, it was another thirty years before Hillary and Tenzing became the first people on earth to set foot on the summit of the mountain, which is revered by the native Sherpas as "Chomolungma"—the highest divinity.

Incredible tales were circulating about Everest. Mountaineers who had come to grief in their attempts to reach the summit were apparently accompanying the summit teams in the shape of silent ghosts. Almost every Everest expedition came back with reports of hallucinations and strange psychic phenomena. Even the normally sober, reliable and experienced Chris Bonington reported in his book *Everest the Hard Way* (1975), a ghostlike figure, which had appeared to Nick Estcourt on the day before a tragic accident. After reading this account, I devoted a great deal of serious thought to these phenomena. Were the ghosts warning us not to cross the last frontier that faces man on earth? Or were Bonington and other witnesses simply succumbing to hallucinations caused by lack of oxygen to the brain? Both possibilities were equally somber. Were we this time pushing our luck too far with our calculated risk? Or would our success again prove us to be right?

Among the few people who, despite all reservations,

Peter Habeler's wife, Regina, with their son, Christian.

all fears and worries, supported us and believed in us unflinchingly, was my wife, Regina. Without the constant encouragement and trust that she showed me at every opportunity during the preparatory period, I would have approached this new adventure with much greater

◁ Peter and Regina Habeler in the Refangebirge (Tyrol).

reservations. If she, too, had doubted us I would perhaps have withdrawn from the whole expedition.

Yet the departure at the airport this morning had shaken me badly. On the trip from Mayrhofen she had sat next to me as if petrified, had scarcely spoken a word but had simply looked at me. And then she had cried and cried, sobbed, and clung to me in desperation.

The memory of this was a bitter spur. I realized suddenly how much I had neglected her during the past months. Months in which I had had only one aim—to train and train, and train again, until I dropped. All that had occupied my thoughts was my one ambitious goal. Poor Regina! If, at the moment of departure, I had given in to my own feelings of tenderness, emotion and bad conscience, I would never have had the strength to leave for this great adventure.

The turmoil and confusion before our departure at Munich Airport jerked me from my gloomy mood. It was March 9, 1978. A few friends were there, plus a few photographers. By chance Freddy Quinn was among the passengers. The photographers wanted to photograph me together with Freddy, but he refused, saying he had never heard of me. I felt insulted. Later when we got talking, he apologized and a little later still, in Frankfurt where I had arranged to meet the other members of the expedition, we were already good friends.

"We have now reached our cruising altitude of 29,000 feet."

The pilot's announcement jerked me back to the present. The friendly stewardess in her blue sari explained in some detail how to use the oxygen mask. "In the event of a loss of pressure in the cabin, an oxygen mask automatically falls from a container above your seat. Press the mask firmly against your mouth and nose, and breathe normally until the airplane has attained a lower altitude."

If the atmospheric pressure on the summit of Everest became too low for Reinhold and me, no oxygen masks would simply drop out of the sky. We had, in fact, firmly decided to work without such a safety net. We would not take any insurance measures and would have no hidden reserves. We wanted to conquer Everest entirely by our own resources.

I was only ten years old when Hillary and Tenzing conquered Everest for the first time, and ever since then this mountain had stood before me like a gigantic distant dream. Just as small boys of today dream of flying to the moon as astronauts, so I wanted to stand on the highest mountain in the world. I had zealously read Hillary's book *Nothing Venture, Nothing Win* as a small boy. Every phase of the assault on the summit stood indelibly engraved in my memory, and when at that time—around the beginning of the 1950s—I began to climb the 9000-foot mountains of my native Austria, I must have already seen myself as a conqueror on the roof of the world.

At barely twelve years of age I had already climbed all the summits of the Zillertal range in the Tyrol solo. When I think today of the dangers to which, through my inexperience, I was exposing myself, it seems to me like an act of providence that nothing serious ever happened to me.

Peter Habeler, aged eleven, in the Zillertal Alps (Tyrol).

Our Everest ascent, however, would be anything but a frivolous, childish adventure. Since 95 percent of the experts considered our undertaking to be doomed from the start, we prepared ourselves far more thoroughly than for any of our previous expeditions. During the first preparatory phase, we were already well aware that we would have to be not only technically and physically in top form, but also that perhaps the most important thing of all was our psychological endurance, our psychological powers of resistance. Lord Hunt, the leader of the successful Hillary expedition, expressed it this way: "Everest exposes the mountaineer to colossal emotional stresses. These stresses can only be borne with unyielding determination and with the iron will to succeed, to conquer."

It would be a lonely struggle. Not only against this sinister mountain and its sinister dangers; not only against physical exhaustion, arctic cold, hurricanes, snow and lack of air; against the treacherous altitude sickness, and the fearful certainty that up there, there would be no possibility of rescue if anything went wrong. But we were also fighting against the heavy burden of wide-eyed skepticism shown to us by friends and enemies alike. When almost everybody believes that what one is planning to attempt is beyond the realms of human ability, then one must either be mad to attempt it or have something within of the spirit of all great conquerors and discoverers, that is unflinching faith in oneself and in success.

Before our Everest expedition, nobody compared us with Columbus, with Scott, with Amundsen, or even with the first astronauts, as people do today. At the most, they called us the "Terrible Twins," and we felt that to be a great compliment. Reinhold and I were considered in the professional world of mountaineering to be people who had "elevated calculated folly to its highest principle," as *Der Spiegel* put it. And others, well disposed toward us, were of the opinion that we had opened up new dimensions for mountaineering. Both opinions are equally false. The precise opposite is, in fact, the truth.

In not one of our undertakings did we ever attempt anything unless we were 100 percent certain of achieving success. We never overestimated ourselves as, alas, so many mountaineers often do, frequently with irrevocable consequences.

Neither of us provoke death frivolously, even if we do allow ourselves to be threatened by it more frequently and have a more personal relationship with it than a man for whom even mowing the lawn amounts to a notable sporting achievement. It is unnecessary to waste more words on this, otherwise one would have to ask oneself why in fact there are any people at all who are willing to gamble for the ultimate stakes.

Our expedition before Everest, the planned first ascent via the Dhaulāgiri South Face in the Himalayas in 1977, ended prematurely. With our limited means, and in the face of the constant dangers of avalanches, we decided it simply could not be conquered. Nevertheless, this expedition, which we had considered to be a preparation for Everest, did provide us with valuable conclusions that we were able to put to very successful use on Everest. One day someone will climb this murderous face, someone to whom the risk is worth less than his ambition, but there will almost certainly be fatal accidents in any such expedition. So much for calculated folly! And as for the new dimensions: We are basically following the old traditions of mountaineers from the pretechnical age. We want to guide mountaineering back to what it should be—a fruitful confrontation of human spirit and strength with nature. We simply refuse to hammer or bore our way up a mountain. We don't want to use any breathing equipment, because breathing equipment allows Mount Everest to shrivel from being a twenty-nine thousander to a mere nineteen-thousander!

One of the Sherpas from Hillary's party expressed it this way: "With oxygen equipment you don't have the feeling of ascending a mountain, you have rather the feeling of descending it." A victory attained by means of technology is for us no victory at all. How can you really test human endurance and skill if you aren't prepared to go to the limit of your endurance?

Reinhold Messner and I arrived by different routes at this same conclusion. That's what brought us together and why we have grown together into a genuine team. We are not friends in the usual sense of the word. We are not "buddies" who stick together through thick and thin. We rarely speak to each other about our private lives. Outside our profession we hardly ever meet; and when we train we do it mostly on our own, and not together. Nevertheless, during the whole history of mountaineering, there have probably never been two men who are as attuned to each other as we are. We understand each other beyond all spoken words. Each of us knows instinctively what the other one will do. Each one can rely 100 percent in any situation on the other. This borders at times almost on the metaphysical. I can still hear, in my mind, sentence for sentence long conversations that we had together during the assault on the summit of Everest. Yet during that time we barely exchanged one word. The dialogues, which Reinhold remembers as well as I do, were never spoken; they simply existed in our thoughts.

I don't need to go any further into the numerous

expeditions we have undertaken together in the Western and Eastern Alps, and later throughout the rest of the world. Reinhold has set this all out in detail in his books, even if the reader may gain the impression from these that he was the leader and I was simply a passenger. However, I don't feel bitter about this—the books sell better that way. The applause of the general public is not so important to me. But Reinhold needs the recognition of that public. He likes to be on public show; he needs the interviews in the newspapers. His birth sign is Virgo, he likes to shine; whereas I'm a Cancerian who crawls back into his shell. I don't like any heroic poses.

There is a photograph that shows me on the summit of the 26,469-foot high Hidden Peak. Reinhold took it, simply because I got there first. This picture was published everywhere with the caption: "Reinhold Messner conquered the Hidden Peak." Friends and acquaintances often ask me: "Why do you put up with this? Have you no ambition? All your common ventures simply become a one-man show for Messner!" Others might have reacted differently—I just let it pass. After all, I would not have reached the summit without Reinhold, and he wouldn't have reached it without me. We are both equally good; neither of us makes a present of anything to the other. The difference lies neither in technical ability nor in motivation, but in our own natures. Reinhold is a more rational man. I am more emotional, and thus we complement each other perfectly.

There is a special reason why I mention Hidden Peak

◁ Peter Habeler in the Wilden Kaiser in 1973 (Tyrol).

The Hidden Peak (26,500 feet).

The Northwest Wall of the Hidden Peak, with the ascent route indicated.

Peter Habeler after the ascent of the Hidden Peak.

at this point. This expedition made Alpine climbing history, and it is what made us finally decide to undertake the Everest venture. The ascent of Hidden Peak in the Karakoram, the Pakistani part of the Himalayas, in 1975, was a pure two-man undertaking. It was probably the smallest expedition that has ever conquered a 26,000-foot mountain, achieved with a minimum of expenditure and equipment, and, what's more, we conquered the summit without using oxygen equipment. This ascent was incredibly tough and difficult. We were utterly exhausted, yet we both felt that we could go farther. This was not the ultimate frontier of what was humanly possible.

I remember it as well as if it were today. After we had overcome all the exertions, all the pain and difficulties that had on several occasions almost forced us to turn back, Reinhold and I sat happily in the plane on the way home. We both ordered a gin and tonic—the height of luxury—and toasted each other, as if we were speaking in unison: "To Mount Everest."

"Without oxygen," I said.

"Without oxygen," came Reinhold's echo. Then we laughed like two small boys hatching some mad prank.

At that time we had no idea how we were going to set about attaining our goal. You cannot climb a Himalayan summit just like that. The 26,000-foot mountains in Pakistan and Nepal are booked up literally for years ahead. There was, therefore, not even the smallest chance of gaining a climbing authorization for Everest from the Nepalese Government before the end of the 1970s. At the moment the mountain is fully booked until the middle of the 1980s. Only experienced and famous mountaineers have the slightest chance that their application will be considered at all. And if, after a lot of bureaucracy, you do manage to get such an authorization, you can consider yourself to belong to the privileged few. An authorization of this type costs, by the way, around $1600. But this item is one of the smallest in comparison to the overall costs of an expedition.

Even in our dreams we couldn't really imagine that we had much chance of getting an Everest expedition off the ground. First of all, we simply lacked the financial means for this. Secondly, and despite our success on the Hidden Peak, we lacked the necessary connections. At best we could speculate and attach ourselves to an expedition that had already been organized and authorized.

In simple terms, we decided we would have to buy our way in.

2

I T WAS COOL in New Delhi in the early morning
hours of March 11. Shivering, we stood around in
the airport building after our landing and carefully
guarded our luggage. Small boys wrapped up in shabby
rugs were begging for a handout, *"Bakshish,"* a look of
practiced entreaty in their eyes. Whole families cowered
on the floor, sleeping while squatting on their heels. Coffee was served out of greasy metal cups, and Dr. Oswald
Ölz from Zurich, one of our expedition doctors whom we
all nicknamed "The Bull," tried out—for the umpteenth
time—the quality of the whiskey he had bought in
Frankfurt. Everybody tried in his own way to kill time
until the departure of our flight to Katmandu. At last we
were finally on our way. We had set foot on Asiatic soil,
and in a few hours we would see the towering chain of
the Himalayas.

Reinhold and I had bought our way into the 1978
expedition of the Austrian Alpine Club under the experienced leadership of Wolfgang Nairz. In 1972 Nairz had
applied to the Nepalese Government for permission to
climb Mount Everest with an official expedition from the
Austrian Alpine Club. His application was granted in

1977, that is to say five years later. This gives you an idea of the length of time needed for planning Everest expeditions. In the meantime, however, Nairz had not been inactive. He had, at least in broad outline, got his team together. The core of this team were his Innsbruck friends, the two doctors, Dr. Ölz and Dr. Margreiter, Joe Knoll, Helli Hagner, Franz Oppurg and others. He had applied for public funds from the Tyrolean Provincial Government. Its chief provincial administrator, Eduard Wallnöfer, was always very understanding about sporting matters, and especially toward alpine ventures of this sort; Nairz, therefore, immediately found a sympathetic ear. The Tyrolean Provincial Government provided considerable funds from their sporting budget. At the same time Nairz applied to industry for support and the relevant firms gladly sponsored the enterprise and provided the necessary expedition material.

Nairz, naturally, also received money from newspapers, journals, radio and television stations. The *Kronenzeitung* took over the largest part of the general expedition costs, along with the *Bunte Illustrierte* and ORF, both the radio and television departments. Reinhold and I were supported in particular by HTV, a private British television company, which wanted to make a film about our ascent without oxygen, and we were also backed by the journal *GEO*.

Without such support from public and industrial funds, a large mountaineering expedition of this type cannot possibly succeed. The cost is so enormous that it is impossible for private individuals to raise sufficient funds themselves, as the following cost sheet will make clear.

Austrian Mount Everest-Lhotse Expedition 1978 of the Austrian Alpine Club

COST SHEET

	EXPENSES	
	ÖS (AUSTRIAN SCHILLINGS)	DOLLARS
1. General costs		
(Authorization, customs duty, gifts, visa fees)	170,000	12,500
2. Organizational expenses		
(Prospectus, writing paper, postage, travel expenses)	60,000	4,412
3. Travel expenses		
Return flight Katmandu	163,000	11,986
Luggage transportation	190,000	13,970
Luggage transportation in Nepal	80,000	5,882
Porters to base camp and back	120,000	8,824
Return transportation of luggage	50,000	3,676
4. Equipment		
New acquisition and replenishment	160,000	11,764
Guide	20,000	1,470
Sherpas (20)	100,000	7,352
5. Provisions		
Base camp	60,000	4,412
High altitude camps	60,000	4,412
6. Insurance		
Participants	36,000	2,648
Guide and Sherpas	42,000	3,088
Radio equipment	10,000	736
7. Wages in Nepal		
Sherpas and guide officer	300,000	22,058
8. Miscellaneous		
Photographic material	20,000	1,470
Medical supplies	10,000	736
Oxygen replenishment	60,000	4,412
Diverse	10,000	736
Minimum reserves	50,000	3,676
Total costs	1,776,000	130,220

Receipts	ÖS	DOLLARS
Own funds raised	500,000	36,764
Ministries	80,000	5,882
Contract Kronenzeitung	200,000	14,706
Contract ORF Film Co.	200,000	14,706
Contract Bunte Illustrierte *magazine*	100,000	7,352
Greeting card campaign	40,000	2,942
Donations from banks and industry	50,000	3,676
Donations by private patrons and promoters	40,000	2,942
Subsidy of the section (of which the individual participants are members)	30,000	2,206
Picture campaign Flora	100,000	7,352
Total receipts	1,340,000	98,528
Deficit to be met	436,000	31,692

This deficit was later met by further contracts with industry as well as by additional donations.

In addition to these general expenses there were also those for personal equipment. This too adds up to a considerable sum. My own equipment was as follows:

3 pairs of long socks
1 LIFA suit
1 sun hat
1 pair of long leggings
1 pair of gaiters to pull over boots
1 pair of climbing boots
1 pair of storm goggles
1 pair of cross-country boots
3 T-shirts
1 dosser (basket) frame with attachment for oxygen
1 rucksack, also to be attached to framework

1   pair rubber bindings
1   pair sealskin-covered skis (for climbing)
1   pair of skis with binding
1   pair of ski poles
1   pair pull-on overgloves
1   insulated thermos flask with 1-quart capacity
1   emergency signal whistle
1   bivouac sack
3   gas lighters
1   all-weather sailing anorak (sort of waterproof parka)
1   climbing belt
1   climbing seat
1   climbing clamp
1   pair of crampons
1   ice ax
1   set of lightweight quilted equipment, consisting of down jacket, trousers, shoes, gloves and sleeping bag.

It must be remembered in all this, that in order to save weight we had reduced our equipment to the indispensable minimum.

Reinhold and I had made a greater financial contribution than the other members of the expedition; moreover, through our connections with industry, we had contributed a larger part of the equipment. In exchange, we negotiated certain privileges. We were thus considered to be a separate summit team, which, as a two-man rope, would be allowed to make the first assault on the summit, a privilege that in expeditions of this kind is unusual. In general, the summit teams are not made up until the actual location is reached, for if somebody is in top form in the Alps it doesn't necessarily mean that he will be suitable for high-altitude climbs.

Reinhold and I had prepared ourselves most carefully

for this bold venture. For the whole winter, and for part of the previous summer, I had trained in the Zillertal mountains. Every day I had exercised for hours under the supervision of my friend, the Mayrhofen ski director, Ernst Spiess. He spurred me on tirelessly. Again and again he urged me: "You've got to move, you've got to move!" This "You've got to move!" was like an inner command. I drew strength from it while on Mount Everest. Even in a condition of complete exhaustion, this injunction drove me ever onward.

My training goals were speed and endurance. I climbed up the Mosele summit in a record time of two-and-a-half hours—and this was on the Ahorn peak as well. Finally, I was in such good form that I put over 3000 feet behind me in thirty-five minutes. Reinhold attained the same form during his training in the South Tyrol. On one of the few occasions when Reinhold and I trained together, we climbed up the North Face of the Eiger in one day, and were back home at our departure point by five o'clock in the afternoon. On this murderous wall, with its highest grade of difficulty, the 6, this was an outstanding achievement never attained before.

Speed of ascent would be the decisive factor if our bold venture was going to succeed. Only if we were in a position to climb through great variations of altitude in record time, would we be able to attain the summit of Everest without artificial oxygen. Only then would we have sufficient energy for one to two attempts on the summit. One essential precondition was that we should adapt ourselves for a sufficiently long time to the altitude; that we should acclimatize ourselves adequately in the base camp and in the various high-altitude camps.

I had never seen Everest before, but I had read all the reports on earlier expeditions most thoroughly. Above all, I had studied in great detail the reports of those Englishmen who, in the 1920s, had almost achieved victory over the summit without any technical support. How primitively these people equipped themselves—they simply wore four or five pullovers, one over the other, woollen gloves, knickerbocker trousers, three pairs of socks and hobnail boots; they put on battered hats and carefully knotted their club ties before crawling out of their canvas tents; their ice axes were large and unwieldy and the thick climbing ropes of hemp sucked up water like a sponge and became intolerably heavy. The very light man-made fibers, of course, had not been invented then. What they carried around with them—on their bodies alone—weighed many times more than our entire equipment.

These reports always gave me renewed strength. After all, if these men with their totally inadequate material had almost conquered Everest, why couldn't we do it with the superfeatherweight equipment that had been especially designed for us; with our shoes of synthetic material and our gaiters; with our warm down equipment and the nylon ropes? Why couldn't we do it?

Nevertheless, we remained cautious in our optimism. We only spoke about undertaking an "attempt" on the summit of Everest without oxygen. We also said that we would immediately abandon our attempts if the experiment should prove itself to be an impossible enterprise. We did not want victory at any price, certainly not at the price of our lives—and not at the cost of our mental and physical health.

We had entrusted the technical part of our expedition to an organization in Katmandu. This firm is called "Mountain Travel," and is managed by Al Read, an old friend of mine from the time I was a ski instructor in America. At that time in Jackson Hole, Wyoming, Al and I had been chasing the same girl, and this somehow made a bond between us. In the meantime, Al had married an American stewardess, settled down in Nepal with her, and opened a flourishing business there. He organizes trekking tours and expeditions. He provides the porters and Sherpas, supplies equipment and books the flights. In short, he sees to everything so that the expedition will be a success. He was our first port of call in Katmandu, and his organization outside the town was the nerve center of our whole undertaking.

I knew Katmandu from an earlier visit; during the Dhaulāgiri expedition I had stopped off—like most of the mountaineers—at the Hotel Shanker. Unfortunately I then contracted a virulent virus infection, which is easily done whenever traveling in Asia. The illness affected me badly, but fortunately did not seriously jeopardize the success of our expedition.

On this occasion, however, I stayed at the Narajani Hotel, which although not so magnificent as the old Shanker, is just as comfortable and clean, and the food was excellent beyond reproach. Moreover, Al had promised to see that we would be looked after with the utmost attention.

It may sound odd, but now in the shabby airport building of New Delhi, while we waited for our connection, I was more preoccupied by potential digestive problems than I was by our distant goal. I had brought with me a bottle of powerful Tyrol schnapps, which has the reputation of being able to nip every illness in the bud pretty quickly, and as a preventative measure I took a fairly large swig of it in Delhi. If I arrive at the base camp in good health, I thought to myself, I need not have any more problems. Up there in the clear cold air, in the bacteria-free surroundings, you are most unlikely to become infected by anything at all. I couldn't know at that time, however, that I would be infected up there on the mountain from—of all things—a tin of sardines, which we had brought with us from Europe, and that our first assault on the summit would be frustrated by this.

Well, who knows, perhaps this infected, tinned food even saved our lives? Now, after the successful completion of our expedition, I sometimes think of this. You see, on that day Reinhold had gone on a short way by himself while I offered up sacrifices to the gods of the Himalayas, and he was to encounter the worst snowstorm of his life.

On that day in New Delhi, the eleventh of March, we were not at full strength. A part of our expedition had already left on the twenty-fourth of February as an advance guard to Nepal. There were only six of us here: Dr. "Bull" Ölz; the second doctor in the expedition, Dr. Raimund Margreiter from Innsbruck; Helmut Hagner, also from Innsbruck; Hanns Schell from Graz; as well as Reinhold and me.

Our connecting flight left finally at ten o'clock, and thirty minutes later the chain of the Himalayas lay before us glistening in the sunshine. The view was breath-

Above, Mani stones (prayer walls), and opposite, prayer flags, with the mantra *"om mani padme hum"* (hail the jewel in the lotus flower).

taking. The mountains looked perhaps somewhat wilder than those of our native Alps but, in fact, they didn't seem very threatening or dangerous. I thought of the rushing mountain rivers, of the source of the holy Ganges, of venerable gurus who were meditating somewhere up in remote caves. I thought of Lamaist monas-

teries and of the strange Mani stones, serving as petrified prayers, hundreds of thousands of which had been erected by the monks in the high valleys. I thought of the photographs that I wanted to take, above all of the children, and I banished far from my mind thoughts of the exertions and dangers that lay ahead. It occurred to me that, for the people who live here, the mountain giants of the Himalayas are gods, and that only about a hundred years ago it was considered an act of blasphemy to set foot on one of these mountain gods. Many of the natives of Nepal and Tibet still have a religious awe of these mountains and of approaching the land of eternal ice, and significantly it is monks who have built their monasteries highest up on the mountain slopes, at an altitude of 13,000 feet, where there is no more vegetation, and where they can be closest to their god.

Katmandu greeted us with heavy rain and with a temperature of about 59 degrees Fahrenheit, which is unusually low for this premonsoon period. Reinhold and I feared the worst. After all, if it was so cold and rainy down here in the valley, farther up it was bound to be snowing heavily. We thought of our expedition the year before on the Dhaulāgiri, which had been brought to a halt by snow and avalanches. At that time we could have no idea that Everest has its own kind of weather, although we did know that the premonsoon period in May, and a short period after the monsoon in September, offer the only possibility of climbing this mountain at all. Furthermore, the Nepalese Government only authorizes expeditions to Everest at these times.

In contrast to many other members of the expedi-

Josl Knoll, one of the members of the expedition.

tion, it was quite clear to Reinhold and myself that we would need a great deal of luck to ascend Everest at all, whether with or without oxygen. Some of our companions considered the mountain to be just one more summit to be somehow clambered up. After all, our equipment was the very best. But in the opinion of Reinhold and myself, these people were far too optimistic, perhaps even somewhat frivolous in their attitude. There was, for example, the Graz entrepreneur Hanns Schell. He collects twenty-two and twenty-six thousanders just like other people collect antiques. He is certainly a good mountaineer, but he equally greatly underestimated the difficulties of Everest. We knew that he of all people would have no opportunity to attack the Everest summit. The same applied to Josl Knoll, who, at fifty-four was the senior member of the team. He felt in top form and hadn't the slightest doubt that he would attain the summit. However, Joe, as we called him, was also destined not to reach the summit, and indeed in the attempt to prove his skill, he would almost lose his life. A third, on the other hand, Reinhard Karl from Heidelberg, whom we had all initially underestimated, was to be the first German to reach the summit of Everest—and he had come with us only as a reporter for the *Bunte Illustrierte,* and without the burning ambition to achieve anything extraordinary.

In general, before the actual departure for the mountain, there was a lot of lighthearted optimism, whereas I was at my very lowest ebb. The small plane, which was to ferry us and our traveling luggage from Katmandu to Lukla—one part of the over 13,000 pounds of expeditionary material had already been sent off in advance by plane—couldn't start because of the bad weather.

I wandered in a very bad mood through the dirty streets of Katmandu, photographed Nepalese children playing in slimy puddles in murky little courtyards. I visited a couple of temples without really taking anything in at all, and felt very sorry for myself because we were unable to make a start. Regina, my wife, had asked me to take home to her something made of silver from Nepal, and although I did indeed search hard for this, I ended up buying nothing. I was so restless and on edge

The famous *Stupa* of Bodnath in Katmandu. Bodnath is a suburb of
Katmandu. The *stupa* is a Buddhist shrine, with the relics of a Buddha,
and is not accessible. The ceremonies take place outside the *stupa*.

that, with the best will in the world, I couldn't adjust to the thought of going home, a return which lay somewhere ahead in the dark future. So Regina is still waiting for her jewelry. One day, however, I will take her with me on a nice, comfortable little trekking tour through Nepal, and I shall enjoy the time and the leisure that I have never had in any of my expeditions.

With Reinhold it was the same. Impatience drove him around restlessly and, like me, he would gladly have set off on foot. We haggled with a few tradesmen because we wanted to buy a Sherpa hat, but we couldn't find one we liked. As if this trivial matter were the most important thing in the world!

I cut myself off from the team, slept a great deal, ate everything that the excellent menu of the Narajani Hotel could offer, and buried myself in two books which I had picked up in Katmandu: *Faces of Everest* by the Indian major Ahluwalia, and the book on the Chinese Everest ascent in 1975, *Another Ascent of the World's Highest Peak* (Foreign Language Press, Peking). I read these books so that, at least in my thoughts, I could be up there on the mountain—that mountain around which all my yearning revolved and which coursed in my blood like a drug.

Market in Katmandu.

The famous five-storied Kumbeshvar Mandir Pagoda in Patan. Patan, which borders on Katmandu, is one of the three royal cities in Nepal. The other two are Katmandu and Bhaktapur.

◁ General bustle at the Hanoman Dhoka (literal translation: Square of the Monkeys by the Gate).

3

URING THE next few days snow fell on the surrounding mountains. Katmandu lies at an altitude of 3936 feet, and the "hills" that surround the Nepalese capital are as high as our highest Alpine peaks. But during this, the warm time of year, they are normally free of snow. Now, in the middle of March, the snow boundary should, in fact, have lain considerably higher. This was a bad omen indeed for our impending long approach march to the base camp at the foot of the twin mountains, Everest and Lhotse.

The sky cleared gradually, and on the fifteenth of March we were told at last that today two airplanes should be leaving for Lukla. By half past six we had traveled by taxi out to the airport and collected our tickets. I was impatient to get away. The inactivity to which we had been condemned in Katmandu was really getting on my nerves. However, in Asia, the fact that one has a ticket doesn't necessarily mean that one is actually going to fly! I knew this from bitter experience, and I therefore shoved myself quite ruthlessly through the waiting

◁ Landing ground in Lukla.

queues with Bull Ölz right behind me. I just had to get away on the first flight. It seemed to me as if my whole salvation depended upon it, and with a great deal of pushing and shoving, Ölz and I managed to obtain two seats in the little Pilatus Porter plane.

Finally, shortly before the landing in Lukla, the summit pyramid of Everest rose up before me for the first time. The view affected me profoundly. What a gigantic mountain! No, not a mountain—a monster. A giant of a mountain. No photo on earth can give even an approximate impression of its primordial power, because one has no comparative order of magnitude. I suddenly became very small and timid. I asked myself if I would ever return from that mountain? Or would the mountain claim me and never yield me up again?

"Inspires respect, Peter?" asked Bull, who with his guttural Swiss accent, bears a marked resemblance to this brute of an animal. He is taller than me by almost a head, rather in the same proportion as Everest compared with the Lhotse.

I merely nodded at his question. Respect was indeed the correct word. Respect was precisely what this mountain instilled in me, and I would always respect it.

With every peak I have ever climbed, I have had a totally personal relationship, as with a friend with whom one is on intimate terms and is an equal, with whom one can measure oneself. But to measure myself against Everest was quite impossible. At no time did this mountain ever lose its sinister and dangerous aspect in my eyes. I could only attempt to approach it with the utmost caution, and perhaps outwit it at a favorable moment. After all, David outwitted Goliath at such a moment. But I would never succeed in really conquering Everest; it could at any time kill me as it had killed many people before me. This became clear to me now, not only from a rational point of view but also from deep within me.

My sense of oppression lasted only a moment; then we prepared to land.

Lukla lies at an altitude of over 9800 feet and is a small Sherpa village, high above the course of the Dudh Kosi River, which has its source at the Khumbu Glacier in the Everest massif. From Lukla we were to proceed on foot to a place about 17,400 feet up, which would be suitable for the base camp. This lay in the morainic slopes of the Khumbu, at the foot of the notorious Khumbu Icefall, which has to date claimed thirteen lives.

Lukla is notorious for its fleas, which seemed to persecute me with particular glee. I can only advise urgently against spending a night in the Sherpa Cooperative Hotel. The finest that Lukla has to offer in its place is a glorious green gentle meadow, the campsite. This site is a sort of caravan serai, and it is here that all the trekking tours and expeditions meet that are en route in this territory. Even for these treks up to the foot of Everest you need an authorization, a so-called trekking permit. But you can get this without difficulty on arriving in Katmandu. After all, about five thousand people a year visit the Everest base camp--quite a considerable number.

On this evening of March 15, a group of New Zealand women had arrived back in Lukla after their tour. There was a tremendous hullabaloo, and in the evening a great dance with the Sherpas round an enormous camp fire. These ladies from New Zealand were mostly of an advanced age, and I was amazed how cheerful they still were, after a doubtlessly strenuous tour. For me, personally, the meeting with the New Zealand ladies was particularly important, because I met Jane Malgrew, the wife of a man who was known to me from books I had read on the Himalayas. Malgrew had had both his feet badly frostbitten during an expedition on the Makālu, and now I heard from his wife (she was in charge of this group of ladies) that his feet had had to be amputated in New Zealand. However, this had robbed him of neither his optimism nor his love of life and, instead of climbing high mountains, he had simply bought a large yacht and had transferred his love of adventure to the sea, organizing spectacular crossings between New Zealand and Australia.

The next stage of our journey was Phakding. Phakding lies about two hours from Lukla. Reinhold and I almost ran the entire stretch. That's a peculiarity of ours. During the approach march to an expeditionary goal we push our bodies to the limit; we want to test whether our training has really achieved its purpose. We hold a regular contest to establish which of us is in better condition. In doing so, however, we are unable to appreciate our surroundings. This is a great shame because I enjoy taking in the beauties of the landscape. During an expedition I am as if possessed; I have eyes for nothing but the goal which is standing before me.

There is no firm road to Phakding, but only a sort of mule track, which rises gently. Here one already begins to feel the affects of the altitude. A competition at this height has nothing to do anymore with mere keep-fit exercises, but is, instead, comparable to a mountain climb in the Tour de France.

The march on foot to the base camp has a second function—acclimatization to the altitude. Let me explain exactly what I mean by this. The higher one climbs, the lower the air pressure becomes, and therefore the less oxygen is pumped into the lungs with each intake of breath. This, naturally, has far-reaching consequences. On Mount Everest the air pressure consists of only one-third of the pressure that exists at sea level. From about 9800 feet on, the oxygen becomes scarce, breathlessness sets in and you start gasping for air. At this stage anybody who is not accustomed to such altitudes will get into difficulties. These include a fear of suffocation, breaking out in sweat, and symptoms of exhaustion—and of course the higher one climbs the worse this becomes. The ill effects don't increase gradually, but rather in a steeply ascending curve. Previously, nobody knew what was the limit of endurance—it was simply assumed that above 26,000 feet it was impossible to exist. Well, Reinhold and I know better now.

The smaller intake of oxygen has a very complicated effect on the human organism. Let us assume that somebody has flown into the Everest base camp by helicopter. That is, as I have already said, 17,400 feet high. Without a gradual transition he wouldn't be able to withstand this altitude. Within twenty-four hours he would be lying in an oxygen tent, gasping for air in a pitiable manner, if indeed he wasn't already suffering from pulmonary edema or a stroke.

Two journalists of the *Stern* magazine visited us in the base camp by helicopter, and owing to bad weather were unable to fly back on the same day. They were very uncomfortable that night, and on the next day needed artificial oxygen. This was because they were not acclimatized to the altitude; they hadn't adapted themselves slowly enough to it. For this reason, helicopter transport into the base camp would already signify the end of the expedition.

You have to ascend on foot, and can only put short daily stages behind you, although for each stage you can push yourself as much as you like, provided you are in good condition. Somebody who allows himself a few days for this ascent is far more likely to adapt to the altitude, and will be well and truly acclimatized when he arrives.

Nevertheless, the danger of suffering from one of the altitude sicknesses is not altogether removed. Above 17,000 feet it is not possible to acclimatize anymore in the actual sense of the word. You can only try over a period of weeks to undertake renewed drives into higher regions so as to accustom yourself a little better to the altitude conditions. But you must descend quickly again. Anybody who stays for a longer period at altitudes above 20,000 feet is hopelessly doomed—perhaps not immediately, perhaps not in one or two weeks, but certainly in the foreseeable future. It depends on the altitude. You may have acclimatized yourself as well as you can; the food and drink can be the very best; you may possess the warmest clothing, the most technically perfect equipment; but eventually the altitude will wear you down, and the higher you are the more quickly this will take effect. Despite sufficient intake of nourishment you will become progressively thinner and more lethargic, and in the end you will simply want to sleep, to drift finally into unconsciousness.

It was for this reason that Reinhold and I found it so important to be able to overcome great altitudes in the shortest possible time. Without oxygen equipment you simply cannot allow yourself a slow ascent. If you haven't succeeded on the third day you must descend, otherwise you are gambling with your life. Many of the earlier Himalayan mountaineers were obviously unaware of the dangers, and consequently they lost their lives. After a thorough acclimatization you must ascend rapidly, and then descend just as rapidly. This was our motto. We had practiced speed at home but, it is true, not under the special conditions of extreme altitudes. The fifty-mile march to the base camp took up a week and meant, therefore, that during this time we were able to acclimatize ourselves thoroughly.

Apart from the mountaineering and climatic difficulties, there were also very important medical reasons why most doctors believe that it is just not possible to climb Mount Everest without artificial oxygen. Since I am not a medical man I will quote here the altitude physiologist Dr. Walter Brendel, who is extremely well known in his profession. Brendel has—theoretically—conclusively proved that Everest cannot be climbed in this way. He explains that the human organism is able to adapt to the smaller supply of oxygen from the atmosphere during a longer stay at altitudes of a maximum of 17,000 feet. Bicarbonate is reduced in the brain tissue.

The sensitivity of the breathing center is thereby increased. This process lasts about thirty-five days. Apart from this, red blood pigment (hemoglobin), which is responsible for the transportation of oxygen around the body, forms at this altitude in increased quantities. In this way it is insured that the body tissue and brain cells can continue to be supplied with sufficient oxygen even under these new conditions. All important physical and mental functions remain intact. If you ascend still higher to the death zone, which begins roughly above 17,400 feet, the human organism simply will not cooperate anymore. A medical experiment of the British Makālu expedition of 1961 had shown that mountaineers who stayed over five-and-a-half months at an altitude of about 19,000 feet had, on the average, lost four pounds of body weight per week, despite the excellent living conditions. Obviously the adaptation limit had been unequivocally exceeded, and from this Dr. Brendel concludes that the higher one ascends above this level of 17,000 feet, the more drastically the time is reduced that one can spend at this altitude without there being lasting damage to the body and to the brain. The reason for this is the lack of oxygen to the tissue. If you add hard physical work to this as well, and after all mountaineering is the hardest and most strenuous work, the time is shortened even more and the tolerance threshold becomes lower and lower. Finally there is a point between 27,000 feet and 29,000 feet where the oxygen intake is sufficient only for breathing and standing, but excludes every other activity. Since in order to survive you need to be able to do more than simply breathe, the tolerable altitude is, in practice, considerably lower. Accordingly, the ascent of Mount Everest without oxygen equipment is physiologically impossible.

Dr. Brendel argues further that through the lack of oxygen, body cells as well as brain cells simply die off. Whereas, with young people at least, the body tissue can regenerate itself, brain cells that have been destroyed are lost forever. As a practical proof of his thesis, Dr. Brendel asserts that English mountaineers who before the war crossed this 26,000-foot barrier without oxygen, came back with very pronounced gaps in their memory. Apart from this "inner suffocation," as this process is called, the lack of oxygen leads to other more serious damage. Your hands and feet become frostbitten remarkably easily, even at temperatures that are not particularly low, because in order to supply the vital inner organs with oxygen, the flow of blood to the extremities is automatically throttled. Further symptoms of how the body reacts to the lack of oxygen include sleeplessness, headaches, vomiting and loss of appetite. And, according to Dr. Brendel, almost the most dangerous thing of all is that: "Mountaineers are themselves often not in a position to recognize the symptoms of incipient danger. Through this lack of oxygen, intellectual performance is severely curtailed, or to put it better, there arises a particular split between the awareness of a danger and the active critical reaction to this danger." And finally: "When reaching altitudes of above 19,000 feet, you should always, on principle, take oxygen with you and, equally on principle, an ascent to the 26,000-foot region should not be undertaken without artificial breathing apparatus. The risk of a mountaineering enterprise lies in the danger of mountaineering itself and not in the overestimation of human powers of adaptation to lack of oxygen."

So much for the opinion of Dr. Brendel, which was set down a couple of years ago. Certainly he is correct in his assessment in one respect: over a longer period of time a stay within this death zone is not possible. But Dr. Brendel ignored one particular thing, and that is the time factor. Both our expedition doctors, Dr. Ölz and Dr. Margreiter, held the view, contrary to Dr. Brendel, that the human organism can indeed tolerate a stay at a height of 29,000 feet, but only for a very short span of time, at most seventy or eighty hours. They were also of the opinion that, although destroyed brain cells cannot regenerate themselves, their functions can, in fact, be taken over by other brain cells. According to Dr. Ölz and Dr. Margreiter a stay at around the 29,000-foot altitude is indeed dangerous, but not necessarily always fatal.

However, one thing I know from experience: mountaineering at extreme altitudes has nothing whatever to do with normal mountaineering. Up there every step is tortuous; every movement becomes savagely difficult. At such great altitudes you become so incredibly tired that it is only with the utmost willpower that you can stay awake—quite apart from the actual climbing!

Incidentally, one thing the scientists have not considered, simply because there are no yardsticks by which to measure it, is that at the absolute limit of physical and mental capacity there is, somehow, an increase of strength—a second wind—which seems to emanate from the innermost soul and which enables the impossible to become possible. I have often felt this, and have always built on it. This important "x-factor" is certainly there, even though I can't explain it or prove it.

4

O N EVERY Himalayan expedition, a doctor is absolutely essential, not only for the treatment of eventual altitude sicknesses, and the constant medical supervision of the mountaineers, but also for the minor complaints. For, after all, mountaineering is not exactly a harmless activity, and the more people who take part in it the greater is the danger that something untoward will happen.

Right from the start we had two medics with us, the surgeon Dr. Margreiter and the general physician Dr. Ölz, and as it turned out their presence was very, very necessary. Especially since, by an irony of fate, one of the patients was to be one of the doctors! Our Bull Ölz.

There were also two bad falls among the Sherpas. Tragically, one of them was fatal. In addition, our Nepalese guide, Mr. Sen, suffered a pulmonary edema, and another Sherpa suffered a stroke, and will probably be paralyzed on one side for the rest of his life. Both doctors are not only medically trained but are also enthusiastic and experienced mountaineers. At least in Bull's case, I wonder sometimes whether he is primarily a doctor or a mountaineer. Bull Ölz was one of the very few who believed firmly in our success and constantly encouraged us right from the start. He used always to hearten us with the words: "If anybody's going to achieve this, then it will be you two."

From the medical point of view, our attempt to attack Everest's summit without oxygen was certainly for him a highly interesting experiment. He brought along with him a number of implements—with which he was constantly analyzing our blood, the red blood corpuscle content—the so-called hematocrit. He would measure, examine and register our kidney discharges, and experimented twice on himself and Franz Oppurg with hemodilution, a method which apparently proved to be very successful on two earlier expeditions.

On our march from Lukla to the base camp we often talked with Bull about this method, in which he firmly believed right up to the experiment on himself in which he nearly died. This technique has to do with the already mentioned capacity of blood to produce increased red blood corpuscles at greater altitudes in order to be able to transport more oxygen. Thanks to the higher red corpuscle content the blood becomes more and more viscous up to a critical point, where it becomes so thick that it can no longer filter through the very fine blood vessels. In the case of this hemodilution, it is a matter, therefore, of tapping off a quart of blood and replacing it with blood plasma. In the process, the blood becomes sufficiently fluid again and can still supply even the finest capillary vessels. This method seems to be obvious enough, but it didn't stand the test in our case.

Nowadays, the Bull goes so far as to dismiss the

whole blood liquefaction theory as complete charlatanry. But, on the other hand, during our expedition he did make one important new medical discovery, namely, that you can counter the thickening of blood to a certain extent if you imbibe as much liquid as possible, that is to say, up to six to eight quarts per day. In the case of Reinhold and myself this was remarkably successful, even if it did demand a colossal effort to drink so much at these altitudes. Your normal thirst is soon satisfied after just one quart, and if you have to drink more, you have really got to force yourself to do it. But through respiration alone an enormous amount of liquid is lost and, furthermore, you sweat abnormally from the tremendous activity. Obviously this loss of liquid must at all costs be replaced, otherwise your body will dry out. In order to replace the lost liquid, only water is available that is obtained by melting ice and snow. This water is similar to distilled water. It contains neither salts nor any other type of mineral material, which the body loses daily through its various secretions. It is essential that this loss be made up, because otherwise the electrolyte balance is completely disturbed. To compensate for that, we took with us a special "electrolyte drink," which we used to take at regular intervals. Let me add that it is incredibly time-wasting and laborious to melt sufficient snow and ice every day in order to satisfy the need for liquid.

I have often been asked why I return from every Himalayan expedition with a full growth of beard. Perhaps this has something to do with the difficulties of preparing hot water at such altitudes? I am asked. Mostly I simply nod and agree, because it is just too wearisome for me to indulge in lengthy explanations. But I would like to take this opportunity to explain the very definite reasons why I always grow a beard in the Himalayas. Firstly, a beard obviously provides excellent protection against the very intense ultraviolet radiation at great altitudes. This protection is not, however, entirely sufficient; even with a beard your face gets badly burnt, so badly that the skin hangs down in strips. Obviously to shave at times like this would be absolutely impossible. Finally, the beard also provides a certain protective warmth. After a day in the open air you find large icicles hanging from your beard—and somewhat resemble a walrus!

I cannot judge whether every member of our expedition was fully acquainted with all these medical problems, but none of them had any ambition to try to compete with us, with the exception, perhaps, of Robert Schauer. He wanted to try to get as far as possible without using any of the oxygen equipment he carried with him. But in the process Schauer suffered such unfortunate experiences that I was almost forced myself by this to give up the whole enterprise. From the height of 23,600 feet on, all of them in any case employed artificial oxygen and slept with oxygen as well.

Reinhold and I passed the first genuine test of our physical condition during our march to the base camp on March 17. In the early morning we marched from Phakding in the direction of Namche Bazaar. That is, Reinhold left the camp before me and I tried to catch up. There's a very beautifully situated path that snakes its way up a ridge back, and that then leads to the left over a large flank. I saw from afar how Reinhold had already put behind him a quarter of the very steep gradient, so I spurted, took some shortcuts and tried to cut him off. But he discovered what I was trying to do and made every effort to beat me. It was like in the old days when we drove each other on to the utmost limits of exhaustion. I knew that on the steep gradients I was quicker than he was, because after a severe attack of frostbite on the Nānga Parbat he had lost a couple of toes.

He is, in this respect, somewhat at a disadvantage compared to me, but, nevertheless, on this occasion I

Namche Bazaar.

Tibetan trader from Namche Bazaar.

couldn't catch up and he was as happy as a schoolboy. I thought to myself. Just look at that! His form is fantastic, this could be interesting. In Namche Bazaar that was some wet, new snow, perhaps four inches deep. The sky

A Nepalese.

was gray and overcast, everything was muddy and dirty, and you sank down ankle deep in the morass.

Namche Bazaar is a Sherpa village, perhaps the best known Sherpa settlement in the Solo-Khumbu territory.

Children from the Khumbu Himal. "Himal" means Snow Mountains.

Here, at an altitude of 13,123 feet a few hundred people still live who have obviously built their whole lives around Himalayan tourism. There is always a colorful throng; male and female Sherpas in their picturesque costumes populate the small streets. There are souvenir shops with silver jewelry and Tibetan carpets, and everything is priced for the benefit of rich tourists. Tea and travel provisions are sold in open halls. Laden yaks stand around and paw the ground impatiently with their hooves. Yaks are a kind of Tibetan cattle that have adapted themselves excellently to the extreme living conditions. They are beasts of burden, providers of milk, and of meat as well. They obviously represent the most important basis of existence for the Sherpas, and during all expeditions they are used to carry the equipment.

Their masters, the Sherpas, are a Tibetan tribe that, in primitive times, settled in Nepal. Sherpas are highly experienced mountaineers. They are brave and strong people, many of whom earn their living by offering their services to expeditions as high-altitude porters and helpers. They have none of the superstitious awe of the mountain that many other Himalayan inhabitants have. Nevertheless, the mountain is still something sacred to them, too.

Our 130 Sherpas, whom Wolfgang Nairz had hired for the transport of our equipment, which had meanwhile grown in weight to eight tons, had dozens of flags printed in a Lamaist monastery with prayers, had them consecrated, and then later hung them up at the base camp on an altar.

As *sirdar*, that is, as Sherpa leader, Wolfgang had

A Sherpa porter. The weight of a load is between sixty-six and eighty-eight pounds.

engaged the well known Ang Phu. He had been on four previous Everest expeditions, and had also been present on the Chris Bonington expedition. This seemed to me to be a very good catch. Nevertheless, the few tensions that later arose during our expedition seemed to originate from Ang Phu. However, to begin with everything went extremely well, and Ang Phu brought the Sherpas with their yaks safely to the base camp and then chose from among his people twenty high-altitude porters and four kitchen Sherpas, who were to help us on the mountain.

A good *sirdar* is absolutely vital to the success of an expedition; a bad one can ruin even the most expensive and well-planned undertaking. Many *sirdars* have become internationally famous, for example Tenzing Norgay, who, along with Hillary in 1953, was the first to conquer the Everest summit. The best of them go up to the highest summits with the *sahibs*, which is what the Sherpas call the white mountaineers; and presumably it will also be the Sherpas who will very soon themselves try to conquer Mount Everest without oxygen.

I am extremely fond of this proud and courageous people with their puzzling and ancient religion, Lamaism, about which even after years of study we Europeans can grasp only the superficial framework. It is a pity that our Western civilization is also beginning to destroy this original and nature-oriented Sherpa culture. In the wake of tourism, even here on the roof of the world, money-grabbing and the profit motive have become established. But, nevertheless, one still finds occasionally selfless hospitality, and it can still happen that one is invited by a Sherpa family to a meal quite by surprise and in the most touching manner.

Although I am very happy to live and work with Sherpas, this time I felt unhappy in Namche Bazaar. Perhaps I was already feeling the effects of the altitude, perhaps I had climbed up here a little too fast. I don't know. What I do know is that I had a headache, I was restless and depressed. The skies simply wouldn't clear, it was cold and there was a draft even in the teahouse in which we were warming ourselves. But a surprise awaited us; we met Wolfgang Nairz and Joe Knoll, who had waited for us here. They had gone on ahead from Lukla and both of them had their wives with them. That was, on the one hand, rather funny, but on the other hand it depressed me somewhat. Shouldn't I have brought Regina with me too? She wanted so much to be with us. But then I abandoned this idea and not without reason. Shortly before my last journey to the Dhaulāgiri, I had canceled all engagements, I had stayed with her at home and had devoted myself to her entirely. We had sat there quietly, listened to music and chatted together. We were particularly close to each other. And then I had asked her: "What would you do if you were in the base camp, and I went up and never returned from the mountain?"

"I would go up and stay with you," she had answered. Simply and in all seriousness. And I had every reason to believe her. We are so attached to each other that one could simply not live without the other. Naturally, Regina would have been delighted with the very delicate silver work in Namche Bazaar. She would have been delighted with the picturesque clothes of the women, and she would have sat for hours with the mountain monks, hearing about their religion and asking them to explain the meaning of the mysterious prayer formula: "*Om, mani padme hum*" (English translation: "Hail, the jewel in the lotus flower.") This is printed on endless strips of paper in their prayer wheels. But, although Regina is a very enthusiastic mountaineer and skier, on the whole our expedition would have been far too strenuous for her. Once again I thought of the scene of our departure. Naturally I had written to Regina in the meantime and told her how much I loved her, and that I would be returning soon in good health. Nevertheless, I was plagued by feelings of guilt.

The next morning, I felt even more miserable. It had snowed; the snow was heaped up in front of our tent entrance and it looked as if we would have to stay here for several days. On seeing the snow, however, the two women decided to turn back, and this allayed my guilty conscience somewhat.

5

THE SUN shone down again from the sky. The snow and the cold were forgotten. My bad mood had evaporated. Before our eyes was a breathtaking sight. Copper roofs and golden pagodas shone in the sunlight and, towering behind it all, covered by a white glistening sugary coat, was the summit of Everest.

Thyangboche, the famous Lamaist monastery, welcomed us. Monks dressed in yellow, their heads shaven, surrounded us and invited us to enter. They wanted to serve us with tea; they wanted to pray for us, and for the success of our venture. Buddha, who rules the four winds, was urged to be merciful to us, and Yama, the judge over the kingdom of the dead, had to be placated. They also invoked the spirits of the dead lamas to accompany us as protection. Sticks of incense were burnt, gongs were sounded, white transparent prayer flags were unrolled and Tibetan tea was served, on the surface of which floated small lumps of rancid yak butter.

Despite the sacred ceremony, I could not force myself to take even one sip of this unpleasant smelling drink. A vague feeling of nausea rose up in my stomach, and I shoved my full cup over to Hanns Schell, who had

already emptied his with a grimace of revulsion. He didn't seem to notice this exchange. However, my punishment followed almost immediately. While I retired for a short time in order to put new film in my camera, the monks handed over to my comrades consecrated

The monastery of Thyang-boche, on the way to the base camp.

The main building of the monastery grounds of Thy-angboche.

white scarves, which were supposed to bring them luck. Only I went empty-handed because I had not been present at that moment.

Although I am not usually a superstitious person, I was nevertheless deeply affected by this, because if you don't receive such a scarf, it is thought very probable that you will never reach the summit of Everest. You alone, I said to myself. I was so gripped by the mysticism of this Asiatic ceremony that I really believed at that moment in the efficacy of these pious gestures. Everybody sat there with their consecrated cloths round their shoulders, and I alone was left an outsider. Naturally, I could have asked the monks to give me such a cloth, and naturally I would have received one. But somehow this would not have seemed genuine.

Lost in my thoughts, I went on with the others in the direction of Pheriche, through the wild mountain landscape, which was bathed in sunlight. Silently we ascended, Everest always before our eyes. After four-and-a-half hours, we had reached Pheriche, a little Sherpa village above the wild rushing Dudh Kosi, a river of melted ice that has its source a little farther up in the Khumbu Glacier. Here we pitched our tents for two days. As is the tradition with Everest climbers, we wanted to pass a certain amount of time here in order to adapt ourselves better to the altitude. The air is already rather thin, you walk slowly, breathing quickly and shallowly, and you really begin to notice the altitude. Nevertheless, cattle graze and people live and work here. The smoke rises vertically from the fireplaces in gentle threads, and when the sun is at its zenith it becomes almost tropically hot,

Khumjung, the largest Sherpa settlement in the Khumbu (12,500 feet).

Potato fields 14,400 feet up near Dingpoche.

because the thin, pure air allows the sun rays to penetrate unhindered. Now it was necessary to protect our faces against the dangers of glacier burns. My beard began to sprout and gradually we were transformed, outwardly at least, into Himalayan climbers.

The last inhabited place at the foot of Everest is Lobuche, a settlement of alpine huts, which are occupied in the pre- and post-monsoon period. Here the yak and goat shepherds live. There is also a rest house in which you can get tea and a simple rice or noodle dish. We reached it after three hours of marching, and pitched our tents.

This last piece of pastureland lies at the edge of the long tongue of the Khumbu Glacier, which is thickly covered by morainic debris.

Our tents stood at the foot of a mountain that towered about a thousand feet above us and, while I was busying myself with the tent I saw two figures climbing about up there. They were the Bull and Joe Knoll, who, for two hours, had struggled up and down the mountain in order to get in some training. Then I too was seized by a similar ambition. My recent defeat by Reinhold really stuck in my throat, and so I spurted up to them, if only to prove something—God knows what—to myself. In fifteen minutes I was at the summit, and after thirty-five

Dingpoche, the highest situated settlement in the Khumbu Himal.

minutes I was back again at my point of departure. Naturally there were spectators, although I hadn't previously told anybody about my intentions. Reinhold, who had observed me, said nothing. Toward evening, however, I saw him creeping quietly and secretly out of the camp. Darkness was already drawing in, so he was unable to go so fast as I had. Now it was his turn to get annoyed, and I could sleep peacefully again. Throughout the time we have known each other, we have always played these little games. It has helped us get faster and faster over the years.

On the next day, the twenty-third of March, we set out at about 9 A.M. We marched over the tongue of the glacier, and around midday reached the base camp, which the vanguard had already set up. A colorful camp city had been erected, and in the background rose up the feared Khumbu Icefall, which anybody wanting to tackle Everest from the Nepalese side has to traverse. This icefall is a genuine death trap. The very sight of it, however, is breathtakingly beautiful. Colossal blue and white ice masses tower up high into the sky. The sun is refracted on the reflecting surfaces and conjures forth color patterns of intense red, green and yellow. But the beauty is deceptive, for the ice is cleft in a most bizarre way. It is broken up in all possible directions and levels, and crisscrossed by dangerous crevasses, which often open of themselves and shut again with a tremendous crash. High towers of ice, so-called seracs, stand apparently firm and then suddenly split and cave in without warning. Whoever happens to be standing or walking under them is doomed without hope of rescue. During the monsoon period, gigantic masses of snow fall on the Everest massif, which collect in the Valley of Silence and form the immense Khumbu Glacier. The pressure with which these snow and ice masses descend to the valley is gigantic. At the lower end of the Valley of Silence the subsoil is uneven; finally it falls precipitously down over a high rock edge. Here the ice collects and towers up, and eventually falls like a frozen waterfall in gigantic blocks down the valley. That is the reason for the sudden and unexpected formation of crevasses, for the collapse of the seracs.

This icefall is like a warning from the mountain to all those rash people who would dare to disturb its peace. "The Khumbu Icefall separates the men from the boys, mountaineers from mere tourists," somebody once wrote, and the image is apt. You can't simply clamber through this ice formation, and then climb up and out at the other end. You have to fight your way through the two-and-a-half-mile long track over a matter of days. When I stood before it for the first time, Dante's Gates of Hell came to me, over which were written the words: "Let him who passes through here abandon all hope." Only in the early hours of the morning, when the frosty night has fashioned the ice to the hardness of steel, can one venture out into this ice desert in relative safety. But even then, however, you must constantly be on your guard for cornices of ice and seracs that break off, and there is just no possibility of avoiding them. Sometimes you hear a sighing and groaning before the thousands of tons cave in, and then you have to make up your mind in an instant whether you are going to run forward or backward in order to escape this danger.

All this, it is true, I knew only from the relevant

literature. Even by summoning up all my powers of imagination, I simply couldn't envisage the reality. But I should say that in all my mountain tours, imagination has been one of the most important reasons why nothing serious has ever happened to me. I can conjure up all the dangers in my mind so vividly that I am automatically looking for ways to avoid them. I believe that the more imagination a mountaineer has, the greater in the long run are his chances for survival. Good powers of imagination are a form of life insurance. But the mountaineer doesn't only need imagination, he needs intelligence; he must be in a position to weigh up the risks. He must be able to judge correctly when an undertaking is pointless, and he must be intelligent enough to turn back at the right moment. This intelligence also includes the ability to evaluate your own strength correctly.

During the bridging work in the large icefall, which is necessary in order to make it, at least temporarily, more or less passable, we, the white *sahibs*, had to lend a hand as well. We could not leave it to the Sherpas alone, because you need alpine experience and alpine shrewdness in order to find the most reliable path through the constantly shifting masses of ice. In order to bridge the crevasses, we used aluminum ladders, which could be connected together up to a length of forty-nine feet. We laid out the fixed ropes, on which we could belay ourselves with a snap-link, and fastened the ropes with some glacier anchors, and ice screws. As always, there existed in the Valley of Silence extraordinarily high fluctuations of temperature. On still and sunny days the temperatures rose at times to over 104 degrees Fahrenheit while at night the thermometer sometimes sank to 31 degrees Fahrenheit below zero. In the process the ice thawed out considerably; as it melted, the surface sank, so that the belaying gadgets came loose and our Sherpas were constantly occupied in seeing to the anchors and the screws and refastening them.

Moreover the great fluctuations in temperature not only made the ice brittle, they caused us considerable headaches as well. In fact they represented the greatest trial to which we were exposed during our whole expedition. During the first night at the foot of Everest I could not sleep at all. I had pitched my tent somewhat to one side—for reasons of comfort, Reinhold and I used separate tents in the base camp—and that night I had taken a sleeping tablet as a precautionary measure. But during the night such a roaring and raging ensued that it sounded like an enormous breaking of surf on a steep cliff. This was the voice of the mountain. The first days on Everest were extraordinarily stormy. The hurricane-like squalls roared in the clefts and ravines; they swelled, they broke and formed howling vortices, and at the same time the glacier cracked and groaned.

During this first night in the isolation of my tent I was overcome by fear. In the face of this primordial force I seemed to myself to be even smaller, to become even more timid than on the day when I had first seen Everest from the plane. How long ago was that? Only a few days. But during that night it seemed to me as if weeks had gone by since I had first entered this threatening world.

On the very next morning I hung up pictures of Regina and Christian, my little son, on the tent pole. Already I felt somehow more at home, more secure. The fear disappeared and gave way to a growing confidence. The work of the day completely pushed aside the fears of the night, my spirits rose and I was once more full of joyful anticipation.

6

Frank Smythe, who in 1933 spent three days on Everest without oxygen at an altitude of over 27,000 feet, once said: "Altitude can change the character of a human being completely. Your friend in civilized circumstances can on the mountain become your enemy. Even his breathing sounds repulsive, his jokes while eating, the noise that he makes chewing, the scarcely concealed triumph with which he always picks out the juiciest delicacies and puts them onto his plate, the ludicrous manner in which he walks, even the cut of his clothing and the color of the patches on his trousers can produce feelings of intense irritation, even of hatred, which are scarcely bearable."

This feeling is well known among mountaineers, and it is precisely for this reason that it is very important to collect together for an expedition people who not only get on well with one another in flat country, but also in the mountains where you are isolated for weeks and become dependent upon one another. Wolfgang Nairz did this extremely skillfully. He took with him only people who had already been together previously on expeditions, and who he knew got on well with one another, even in extreme situations.

Now in the base camp we were all together at last. First of all, there were our two expedition doctors, Dr. Margreiter and Dr. Ölz. Dr. Margreiter is an extremely conscientious man, whose qualities as a friend were already well known to me as a result of an expedition in South America in 1969. He is an honest man, who always expresses his opinion clearly and openly, regardless of whether or not it will please his companions. He is completely uncompromising. With Reinhold he would get into very lively and sometimes rather sharp discussions. These two are at completely opposite poles in their political and social opinions. Dr. Margreiter is what you might call a radical conservative. He is deeply religious and his family means everything to him. As a mountaineer he is equally hard and consistent. He had prepared himself excellently for the expedition, and for that reason I am extremely sorry that he didn't get to the summit with us. I would have wished it with all my heart. He was, by the way, one of the few who always believed in us unconditionally.

Bull Ölz is a completely different person. He looks like a hippie with his long beard, and at first sight one would never take him for a doctor. In spite of this he is completely devoted to his profession—he is a medical man body and soul. On the other hand, he is not by any means a one-sided person; he is extremely versatile and knowledgeable in a number of areas. He is a great lover of music and of art. He is a gourmet and he is a passionate mountaineer, who knows the highest summits in almost all continents. Bull is a grand man with whom I always got on extremely well during our Everest expedition. He

Dr. Raimund Margreiter, one of the two expedition doctors.

Dr. Oswald Ölz, nicknamed "The Bull," the second expedition doctor.

is honest and he always says what he thinks. He is fair and tolerant, and he never says anything to wound. What distinguishes him particularly is his modesty; where matters concern him personally he understates rather than pushing himself into the foreground. When we arrived at the base camp he had three dream goals. The first goal, Mount Everest, he has now attained. The second goal is to possess his own clinic, and the third is to have a really select wine cellar. In this area also he is a connoisseur. I have already mentioned that he had laid in in Frankfurt the best whiskey and cognac brands, so that he wouldn't go thirsty on the mountain.

Horst Bergmann is a car metal worker and cameraman. Thus, he too, is a versatile man. He is an excellent cook and also the most skillful with his hands amongst us. If there was any technical problem, Horst always solved it. He made a decisive contribution to the victory of the first summit team, because he was extremely *au fait* with the equipment for oxygen inhalation. You could always have a good discussion with him because he would never get stuck in any fixed dogmatic opinion. He is, by the way, also an excellent kite flier.

Hanns Schell, the Graz entrepreneur, is a man to whom success is most important. He was consumed by the ambition of taking home with him, in addition to his two previous 26,000-foot mountains, a further one. How he was going to do this was relatively unimportant. Hanns Schell is particularly good at organization. He contributed a great deal in the preparation for our expedition, but unfortunately he was very unlucky because the Sherpas boycotted his ascent to the summit. As a mountaineer he has a completely different rhythm to Reinhold and myself. During all ascents he would take two or three times the amount of time that we thought appropriate. But he is single-minded and persevering, and he almost always attains what he wants. Even on Everest he never let up in spite of his lack of success. I have heard that he has bought himself into a Yugoslavian expedition, which is undertaking this same tour next year. He is, incidentally, already over forty years of age, which is a considerable age for such excursions.

It seems that a mountaineer has reached the height of his potential around his midthirties. This differs from other types of sport where you are already going downhill after the age of twenty-five. The reason for this is that a good mountaineer needs not only physical strength and good condition but, above all, experience. And you only acquire experience after a number of years. An exception to this rule was Robert Schauer, who was, at the age of twenty-four, the Benjamin of our crew. In spite of his youth, he is an excellent man with far-reaching ambitions. In my opinion, he alone—apart from Reinhold and myself—would have possessed sufficient strength and motivation to get to the top of Everest without oxygen. For this reason I was deeply upset when Robert, after his own first attempt, categorically declared: "It is not possible."

Helmut Hagner from Innsbruck is a man whom I, as chief of the Austrian mountaineering guide training scheme, know very well. He is one of the most experienced and careful mountaineers that we have. He earns his living as a mountain guide, that is to say he is a professional mountaineer. A victory over Everest would certainly have greatly confirmed his reputation. But he, too, was a victim of the Sherpa boycott. He unjustly blamed Nairz for this. He was desperately disappointed about the failure of his enterprise. During the last few years Helmut has had a great deal of bad luck. Perhaps the reason for this lies in the fact that he doesn't want success strongly enough. He is not a fanatic, but is rather a moderate in pursuing his goals. This makes him a good teacher and a good guide—but also makes him a loser on the mountain.

Our expedition chief, Nairz, is a fascinating personality. Nothing can shake him from his phlegm and calm, and he always gives the impression of being very casual and composed. But when necessary, he always gives 100 percent of himself. He works precisely and very effectively. Thanks to his high intelligence, it is easy for him to cope with the complicated organization of a mountain expedition. This would present anybody else with considerable difficulties, myself included. Nairz possesses a great deal of intuition and he is extremely skillful at settling differences of opinion. After our expedition he was reproached for having taken Ang Phu with him as a summit Sherpa. Once Ang Phu had got to the top of Everest, according to Nairz's critics, his interest in the expedition rapidly declined, and this prevented the rest of the team from reaching the summit. But I believe that in Ang Phu, Nairz made the correct choice. Ang Phu is strong and ambitious. He has the Sherpas well under his control and has always proved himself an ideal leader. It is thanks to him that any of our group at all reached the summit.

Wolfgang Nairz works in the Austrian Alpine Club, and a short while ago took over a responsible position there. For us he was the ideal expedition chief; we couldn't have imagined a better one.

Our senior member, Josl Knoll, is a real old bear. He has a lot of experience in the mountains; among other things he undertook a trip with Hermann Buhl. But he never ventured on really difficult tours. He only took part in our expedition out of friendship for Nairz.

Then there was Franz Oppurg. He serves as a professional soldier in the Austrian Army and is a simple, straightforward man and a good comrade. He has had brilliant successes in the Alps, but on Everest he had a great deal of difficulty with the altitude because too many red blood corpuscles were forming in his body. Bull, our doctor, treated him then with the hemodilution method, but this lasted for only two days. He dragged himself painfully from high-altitude camp to high-altitude camp, and it was only when he started using artificial oxygen that his condition began to improve.

Reinhard Karl, the reporter for *Bunte Illustrierte,* was the only one whom nobody knew previously. As an outsider, initially he had great difficulties with us, as we did with him, but we had all misjudged him. By the end we became firm friends. His greatest difficulties were with Margreiter, because he always liked to help himself first when there was something good to eat. Reinhard reminded me somehow of a lonely wolf who had first to become accustomed to us, this alien pack. Nevertheless, he is one of the best German climbers and an excellent photographer.

Two cameramen from the British television company HTV took part in our expedition. This company had also provided a part of the funds with which Reinhold and I financed our expedition contributions. The only task of these two cameramen, Eric Jones and Leo Dickinson, was to film our ascent without oxygen. Eric is a well-known English mountaineer, very ambitious and methodical, but not a particularly fast climber. On the other hand, he is uncommonly tough. It means nothing to him to spend a night at great altitudes in the open air. Somehow or other he manages to find a crevice in the rock, crawls into it, and then the next morning crawls out, taps the snow from his clothes and goes on climbing. I believe Eric is a lonely man. Although he fits into any company, he nevertheless goes his own way without ever showing his cards. I like him very much, and I could well imagine living weeks with him in a tent without any conflicts flaring up between us.

Dickinson is the complete opposite of his friend Jones. He is a clever, lively, extroverted man with a typically English dry sense of humor. If ever tension threatened, Leo was there and quickly relaxed the atmosphere with his jokes. He is a crazy filmmaker, with brilliant ideas and inspirations, always searching for remote perspectives and unusual angles from which to photograph. During a hair-raising journey through the Himalayan rapids, he once mounted his camera on the bow of his kayak. In the process he took a series of pictures that were quite fantastic and unlike anything anyone had seen before.

And now let me add a few words about my partner, Reinhold Messner. I have known Reinhold for over fifteen years. We were introduced to each other by a common acquaintance. We undertook a few individual mountain tours together in the Alps and became friendly. The decisive thing was that we both possessed the same attitude to alpine climbing. For us it was a matter of taking mountaineering back to its natural forms. We had a low opinion of the purely mechanical technique with which the mountaineers of the 1960s simply nailed and hammered their way up the steepest walls. We wanted, on the contrary, to breathe new life into the original adventure of climbing. We had arrived at this attitude by independent routes, both of us in a way pioneers of a new trend. Since our success has proved us right in our belief, our type of mountaineering is gaining more and more supporters and disciples. When I first met Reinhold he was a sociable, likable fellow, firm in his character and beliefs, but not at all touchy. I feel that since the great Nānga Parbat expedition of 1970, his innermost personality has undergone great change. During this expedition his brother was killed, and many of Reinhold's critics blamed him for this tragedy. I know that this reproach is most unjust. Nevertheless, it hurt Reinhold very deeply. For years he wrestled with this question of his own guilt, and perhaps even today has not yet come to terms with it.

During the Manāslu expedition of 1971 two more people were killed. Once again, people started blaming Messner, in my opinion equally unjustly. One of the two men, Jäger, who undertook the assault with Messner, simply couldn't keep pace with Reinhold—he lagged behind him and descended to the last camp, while Reinhold continued the attack on the summit. Jäger never reached the camp. In the search for him, another man, Schlick, was also killed. The attacks which followed this second tragic event were even more vehement. Reinhold's opponents went as far as to assert that anybody who went on a climb with him ran the risk of being killed. Reinhold defended himself against these accusations, but he had to defend himself entirely alone. He received no support. This may have made him inwardly very hard, may even have embittered him. He also discovered on this occasion the power of the press, the power of journalists, and he learned how to use them for his own ends.

Reinhold is a master of public relations; he is brilliant at handling the media and their representatives. This never disturbed me. On the contrary, Reinhold's public controversies drew us even closer together. Messner found in me a partner upon whom he could rely completely; one whom he didn't have constantly, like others, to keep an eye on or worry about. On the mountain we are as one man; we think as with one mind, and we are literally inseparable. This inner hardening, this embitterment has, I think, made Reinhold Messner a very lonely man. Loneliness is his great problem. Unlike myself, living together in Mayrhofen with my old friends from my childhood and boyhood, and with whom I still sit down and drink, Reinhold has destroyed the bridges connecting him with his past; he has completely dissociated himself from it. He has separated himself from his earlier friends, even from his wife.

During this period of increasing loneliness, Reinhold began to write. Yet in his books he seems to me to be quite a different person from the one that I have known in person. It is, in fact, impossible for me to characterize this man accurately. His has a many-faceted personality. He is predictable, always wanting to move on, and always searching for something new. Seen in this light, Everest is only a transitional period for him, one stage among others in his life. Many people say that Messner is greedy for publicity, that he is hooked on applause and always wants to be the center of attention. I have the impression that he was somehow forced into this role by the mass media, who need a new victim every day. It may be that in the meantime this role has come to suit him, but nevertheless I am convinced that the first push in this direction did not come from him personally. As I have said, it is impossible for me to do justice to Messner, even approximately. Although I have known him for fifteen years, and in my opinion know him better than many people from his closest circle of friends, he remains for me a complete enigma.

There is one thing I would like to stress: throughout the many years we have been together, and during all the adventures we have shared, the dangers and difficulties of which cannot properly be estimated, Messner has always proved a very loyal friend to me. He is always in harmony with me, as I am with him. No harsh words have ever been uttered between us. We have never had an argument, or any great differences of opinion. There has always seemed to exist between us a silent understanding, a phenomenon that I cannot really explain even to myself, but which is the very essence of our success.

7

ACCORDING TO our plan of action, once we had crossed the icefall and secured our route through the Valley of Silence, we would attack the main summit via the south pillar. To do this, a number of high-altitude camps had to be set up above the base camp. The stretches between the individual high-altitude camps had to be secured for the Sherpas, if possible with fixed ropes, so that with their loads of up to forty-four pounds in weight, they could cross without difficulty over the dangerous traverses.

Normally you set up six altitude camps on Everest. The first is at the end of the icefall at an altitude of about 19,000 feet; the second at 21,000 feet at the foot of the Everest southwest wall; the third, according to the chosen route, on the south pillar or on the Lhotse Face, at an altitude of 22,000 feet. The fourth camp then lies at about 23,000 feet, directly in front of the South Col of Everest; a fifth camp, 26,000 feet high, is at the South Col. Finally, Camp VI, at 28,000 feet, is set up directly at the foot of the South Summit, and it is from here that the assault on the summit normally follows.

The camps are set up one after the other, the teams

Left to right: Dickinson, Messner and Dr. Ölz on the approach to the base camp.

ascending in alternating shifts and returning to the base camp once their work is complete. They sleep both on the trip out and the return trip in the camps that have already been set up. This constant up and down, to and from the base camp is necessary, because above 18,000 feet you are already in the death zone in which your physical strength rapidly wanes. Recovery from this is only possible in the base camp, which lies below the death zone. Here you can rest up for weeks, whereas the stay in Camps V and VI, even with the aid of oxygen equipment, must be restricted to only a couple of days.

As soon as Camp VI has been erected, the predetermined first summit team climbs from the base camp swiftly up through the individual camps, where adequate provisions, medicaments, stoves, fuel and oxygen bottles are stored. After one night in each of the high-altitude camps, the summit team reaches the summit no later than the sixth day after its departure, so that within three days it can descend again to the base camp. It is then the turn of the second summit team, followed by the third, until as many members of the expedition as possible have reached the summit. This was our plan in theory. However, we were not yet able to calculate how far it would have to be modified.

On our day of arrival at the base camp, our comrades from the advance party told us: "There's much too little snow on the ground this year, everything is bare ice. It will be very difficult."

"Difficult" was, to say the very least, an understatement. However, we only discovered this for ourselves a few days later, for first of all we had to organize ourselves in the base camp. We unpacked our equipment and sorted it out. This took three days, up to the twenty-seventh of March. By then, Oppurg and Schauer with the three Sherpas had already bridged the first third of the Khumbu Icefall with metal ladders and ropes. They told us of avalanches and glacier crevasses, which forced them constantly to retreat and take new routes. Time passed very slowly, and we longed for some snow. But Everest has a mind of its own as far as weather is concerned, and is completely unpredictable. The mood in the camp was one of depression, and from day to day the curses uttered during the extended card games became more and more earthy. Everybody was letting off steam in order to fight the mounting frustration. Also, much to our annoyance, a few containers with pieces of equipment had not yet arrived. Thus, Dr. Margreiter, Hagner and Nairz were still without their climbing boots and were, therefore, temporarily ruled out of the work in the icefall. The inactivity in the base camp was getting on our nerves.

Thank God the weather was pleasant enough. During the day it was quite warm; at night, on the other hand, the temperature fell to 13 degrees below zero Fahrenheit, which for this time of year was much too cold. In the Sherpa kitchen the wooden log fire was burning the whole day. Ice was melted and hot water prepared for bathing and for making tea. We sat in the bathtubs in our tents, wallowing around luxuriously in the warm water, and then lay out in the mountain sun. Sherpa women brought new stocks of firewood from the valley. Even from afar we could see the slender figures in their long colorful clothes. Wood is rare up here and therefore expensive. One bundle, enough for about half a day, costs 15 rupees (about $1.50). Calling out and laughing, the girls approached the camp, unloaded their burdens with the "kitchen boys," and then disappeared without further ado into the tents of their male compatriots. There the giggling continued, which provoked many a sugges-

tive remark from us. Obviously the Sherpas are very free and easy in their love life, and I have often asked myself how they establish who in fact is the father of a baby!

There were two large fireplaces in the base camp. One belonged to the Sherpa kitchen where our Sherpa team, now reduced to twenty-four men, catered for themselves, while we were catered for in the *sahib* kitchen by the kitchen Sherpas. We had such varied dishes as yak meat with rice or rice with yak meat—if, that is, we got yak meat at all. The slaughtering of animals is forbidden here for religious reasons, being so near beneath the seat of the gods. Once, therefore, we had a yak slaughtered down in the valley. It must, however, have been a pretty ancient bull, because the meat was as tough as old leather. But I must not be unjust; the cooks really gave of their best and put in a lot of effort to prepare something tasty from the meager supplies they had.

Eating was after all our main activity; we had, as it were, to fatten ourselves now, since in the high-altitude camps we would scarcely get up an appetite. Breakfast was at 9 A.M., and then toward 11 A.M. came a light snack, and at 1 P.M. the main midday meal was ready. At 5 P.M. we had high tea with tea or coffee and bread, and at 7 P.M. the warm evening meal was served. In the meantime, if there was nothing else to do and we were not on the duty roster or reconnoitering or doing bridging work, we passed the time sleeping, reading and making excursions into the immediate vicinity.

◁ Two female Sherpas from Pangboche in the Khumbu Himal.

I took a lot of photographs, I read and listened to music, which annoyed the otherwise peaceable Horst Bergmann. The violin concerto by Puccini, which I love so much, was the object of such loathing to him that, after about two hundred playings of the tape, he used to creep around my tent with an evil look on his face and an ice ax held threateningly in one hand. He couldn't be pacified, even with performances by Reinhard May, and in the end was unable to bear my music at all! And this even though I had prudently erected my tent somewhat to one side. Because of Bergmann's allergy toward music, I managed in the course of time to read right through Mao's *The Long March,* and also to study over and over again the mountaineering books that I had brought with me. Only the meal gong disturbed me in my meditation.

"Good morning, sir, early morning tea."

The voice of the kitchen boy woke me on the morning of the twenty-eighth of March from my dreamless sleeping-tablet slumber. Now, at last, Reinhold and myself were given the green light to go. For the first time we climbed up to the icefall. There was a lot of hard work ahead of us. Sherpas followed, carrying up ladders and ropes, and we gradually ascended through the already bridged part of the glacier.

Now, for the very first time, we became aware of the dangers of this icy hell. Bizarre rubble and debris, in parts thousands of tons in weight, blocked our way. Great yawning crevasses opened up before us; the dangerously leaning seracs rose up to the skies. Ladders from earlier expeditions lay bent and smashed beneath great broken pieces of ice. Thousands of square feet of the subsoil must have broken up and fallen into the depths. The glacier was like a living being. It cracked and roared, and the wind howled in the ice crevices. We bridged part of the way and then returned to the camp. To spend the night in this dangerous terrain would have been extremely stupid. On the thirtieth and thirty-first of March we worked desperately and silently. We fixed *névé* (old, partially-packed snow) anchors, fitted ice screws, stretched ropes and laid out ladders, and then collapsed into our tents at night almost dead with fatigue.

In spite of the tremendous physical exertion, I found it difficult to sleep during these nights. I was plagued by headaches. I was restless, and sweating a lot. Each morning came as a blessing. The optimism of the others, who seemed to believe that they would conquer the summit without much difficulty, amazed me more and more. As far as I was aware, there had never been an expedition in which all the participants firmly believed that they would get right to the summit of Everest. Generally, it is considered a success if even one rope gets safely there and back again. Yet the weather continued to be good; there were neither storms nor great avalanches, and during the day the sun burnt down so strongly on the camp that we took off our warm eiderdown clothing.

Reinhold Messner was no more optimistic than I was. Both of us still remembered vividly the horror of the Dhaulāgiri South Wall, when storms and constant avalanches had finally worn us down and forced us to retreat. Equally, we had not forgotten the exertions of Hidden Peak, where we had struggled desperately to get to the summit. Once again our exhaustion was so acute that on more than one occasion we were tempted to give up and turn back.

It is in the upper region that the icefall is at its most dangerous. It seemed a miracle to us that, apart from a few scratches and abrasions, there had not been any serious accidents. The mountain had been keeping quiet, but soon it would strike—this I sensed with every nerve of my body. My unease grew, and I urged more haste.

On April 1, Reinhold and I had conquered the ice labyrinth. We stood happily in front of the Valley of Silence, which Mallory had dubbed with the Welsh name "Western Cwm" (western valley). On the right, the iced flank of the mighty Nuptse towered up; on the left, the western shoulder of Everest, on which colossal ledges of ice were hanging, threatening to break off at any moment. The whole valley presented itself to our eyes as a wasteland of ice and snow, threatened constantly by avalanches and collapsing ice. I had little feeling for the majestic beauty of the view at this moment. I thought only about our task, of the lonely struggle against snow, ice, lack of air and fatigue, which lay ahead. The summit, which stood so close to me that I could almost grasp it, seemed to me farther away than ever. Together with two Sherpas who had accompanied us, we pitched two tents and announced our success to the base camp over the radio. Great cheering answered us. The path was clear; the actual attack on the mountain could begin.

Our two tents were basically not designed for high-altitude conditions. They were not secure against storms, and I had many fears that the rising wind would tear them to shreds during the night. But thank God they held firm.

Battered and exhausted, we crawled out of our sleeping bags the next morning very late, and continued to make a trail. The sun burnt down on the valley, and the temperatures rose quickly to over 86 degrees Fahrenheit. Painfully, we pushed forward and toward one o'clock we reached the site where we wanted to erect our Camp II, the later so-called "advanced base camp."

A great disappointment awaited us. The south pillar, over which we wanted to try the ascent, was as smooth as a mirror and free of snow. Reinhold radioed to the base camp: "No decision has yet been made, but we have established that the climb to the south pillar has shown up green, bare ice, and we are almost certain that none of the Sherpas will have the technical ability to climb up over this south pillar with provisions for us in the camps. On our own we are simply not capable of doing this. We will probably, therefore, be taking another route, via the Lhotse Face, and from there will have to climb up to the south pillar, in order to go on up to the last camp."

The storm got more violent, and dark clouds rolled down to the valley. Our two Sherpas' faces looked rather doubtful, but finally they set off as quickly as possible on the return trip to Camp I. Ahead of us lay one of the worst nights that I have ever experienced. The mountain was beginning to take up arms against the intruders.

8

I T WAS NOW time for us to pitch our tent. The storm had risen to a hurricane, raging and howling, so that we could barely make ourselves heard. Like hunted men, we hacked away a small space for our tent. The storm literally ripped the tent awnings out of our hands. Only after tremendous efforts did we succeed in erecting the tent poles and pinning down the tent. The icy wind whistled through the tiniest slit and blew in quantities of the finest snow powder. The tent poles bent as though they would snap, and at any moment our airy accommodation threatened to be torn to shreds.

The hurricane became worse and worse. Toward five o'clock in the evening, I struggled outside in order to fix both ridge pieces with a climbing rope. The squalls threatened to rip the rope out of my hand, but somehow I managed it and crawled back into the tent. I was seized by a fear that would not let me alone. If the tent was blown away, or torn up, we had no chance of survival. In the dark we would have to hack a cave out of the hard ice with our axes in order to crawl in and huddle closely together in our sleeping bags. From reports of previous expeditions, I knew that scarcely anybody had survived such a night in the open air. Was this already the end? With a ski pole I tried to strengthen the tent poles, which were bending in all directions. Yet, even if the tent did hold, what would happen on the next day if the weather did not improve, and we were trapped by fog?

I thought of the English expedition that, in 1971, had been imprisoned here for ten days and nights in storm and fog. Their supplies were used up, and freezing conditions and lack of oxygen had reduced them to a state of total exhaustion. They were rescued literally at the last minute. John Cleare, who was on the expedition at that time, had told me in detail about it. Reinhold and I, on the other hand, hadn't even got sufficient food with us, and the yellow marker flags, with which we normally marked out the route, had not been fixed yet. If we had turned back, we would have lost our way hopelessly in the storm and fog; under no circumstances would we have found the return route to Camp I.

It was a serious situation that caused me a great deal of worry. Reinhold pretended to be much calmer than I was, but his stoical attitude did not reassure me at all. It may be that I have an essentially sharper instinct for weather conditions than he has, an instinct that on frequent occasions has already stood us in good stead.

Somehow, however, the night did pass. The storm abated a little at daybreak, and I urged that we should turn back. It was five o'clock in the morning on the third of April. We were so weakened by two sleepless nights and the cold, that we stumbled rather than walked back. For the return journey to Camp I, which we later put behind us in just two hours, we took almost twice as long. The altitude, the storm, the cold, and the exertions of making a trail through the deep snow, had sapped that strength of which a few days previously I had been so proud.

Looking back, I saw Everest between the suddenly opening clouds. A long trail of snow drifted from its summit, as if in mockery or as a farewell. It no longer seemed important. It was a matter of complete indifference to me now whether I ever got up to the top or not. My senses were dulled; even my sense of danger had disappeared. I moved only automatically. And then, almost without warning, the wind dropped, the clouds disappeared, and the sun burnt down. If before we had been frozen cold, now we boiled under the pitiless heat.

If somebody had said to me at this time that I would soon ascend again, that I would soon expose myself to even greater exertions, and would go on doing so until I stood at the top, I believe I would have thought he was insane. What was going on in Reinhold's mind, during these hours in which we were looking for the way back to Camp I, I don't know. But his thoughts can't have been very heroic, because he was just as shattered as I was.

After three-and-a-half hours we were in Camp I, and, after a short stay, we descended immediately to the base camp. The colorful tents and the life of the camp made me forget instantly the trials that I had just overcome. I felt as if I were returning to a cozy, warm home.

However, the experience of this stormy night also had a positive side. I had seen that the grinding fears were unnecessary; that, on Everest, things happen differently than they do on other Himalayan mountains, where the weather often stays bad for weeks on end once it has begun to get stormy and to snow. After nights in which we hadn't had a wink of sleep because of the roaring and howling of the hurricane, suddenly the sun shone again and the world was bright and friendly; everything was as it should be once more. The Everest territory is distinguished in particular by these sudden fluctuations in its weather.

On the seventh, eighth and ninth of April, we pampered ourselves in the base camp. Mail arrived from Regina, my wife—a tremendous thrill that finally restored my spirits again.

I saw the mailman from afar, a seventeen-year-old lad who regularly came up from Lukla. While we all surrounded him, I immediately recognized Regina's handwriting. Then I retired to my tent, crept into my sleeping bag and read the letter. Up here, where you are cut off from the whole world, mail plays a very important role. Everybody longs for some message from home. When the postman comes, even fully grown, tough men behave like children. They rush toward him and almost tear the letters from his hand, and then retire with unconcealed triumph if there was something for them. It was the same with me, and if ever there wasn't any mail for me, I was overcome by a deep sense of disappointment. Whenever possible, I wrote back immediately to Regina.

The weather was so bitterly cold that the condensed water on the inner walls of my tent froze. I wrote by candlelight, with gloves on my hands, hoping my wife would be able to decipher my illegible writing.

After three days in the base camp, we had completely recovered. We once again discussed which route

From left to right: Knoll, Nairz, Messner and Habeler at the base camp.

we were going to take, and decided that the south pillar was impassable. There was nothing left for us but to take the route of the first climbers, that is via the Lhotse Face. Now we were really aching to go up again to secure the new route. Camp II had become a cheerful sort of tent city in the snow, and served from now on as the advanced base camp for the summit teams. I was relieved when, on

April 10, Reinhold and I set off as a two-man rope. After a few days of sitting around inactively we were full of impatience; we just had to get on with the job now, just had to do something. The old goal stood before us as temptingly as it had at the beginning of our trip. I felt myself to be in great form.

We climbed through to Camp II, and on the eleventh of April we were already on the Lhotse Wall. Once again we were entering virgin territory, because up to that point none of our team had been up here. It was our task to find a safe place for Camp III, to set up the first tents and to provide the track leading to it with fixed ropes. We belayed the iced wall and were able to use, as a means of orientation, the ropes of earlier expeditions who had chosen the same route. It was a damned difficult job in this bare glacial ice. We could only move forward on the front points of our crampons. Everywhere the wind had blown away the layer of snow, so that progress was slow.

We decided to leave out the traditional site for Camp III on the Lhotse Face, because there seemed to us to be too great a danger of avalanches there. But we didn't have enough rope with us to belay everything up to the posi-

•

Pages 108–109
Aerial photograph of Mount Everest. The line marked __ __ shows the originally planned ascent route; the line __.__.__ is the route chosen later via the Lhotse Face. In the foreground is the Valley of Silence. Camps II, III and IV are shown.

Pages 110–111
Map section of Mount Everest territory. The route from the base camp through the Khumbu Icefall via Camps I, II, III, IV and V to the summit is indicated.

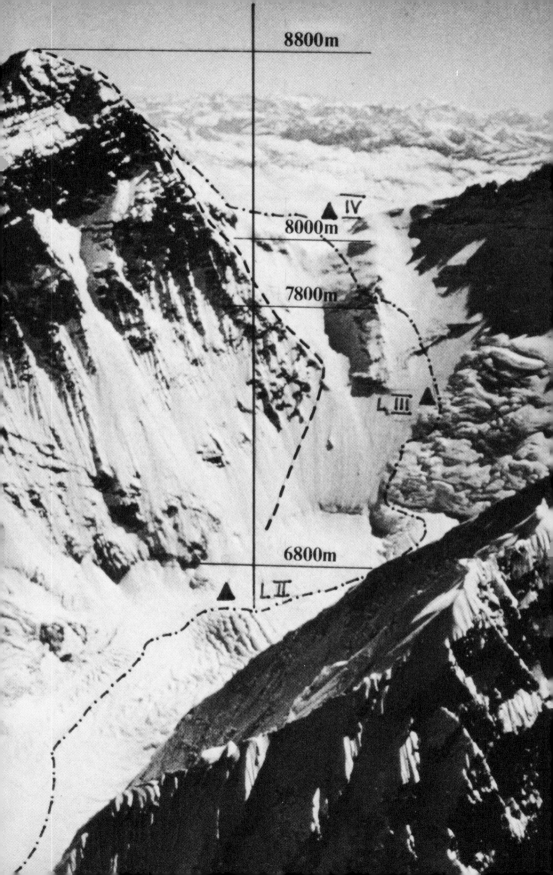

tion of the next site, Camp IV, at an altitude of 23,600 feet.

So once we had used up all our rope, I descended again, from an altitude of nearly 23,000 feet, while Reinhold went on with a couple of Sherpas another 650 feet to where he could reconnoiter the terrain.

I waited for him in Camp II. He told us that up there he had come across the remains of a Korean tent and that the site was very well suited for our Camp III.

On the next day it was very hot; the thermometer climbed up to 108 degrees Fahrenheit in the shade. We ascended the ice wall again, dressed only in shirts and pullovers, in order to make it passable up to the planned campsite for the high-altitude porters and the rest of the team. We hung in more rope, improved the belaying of the day before, and after everything had been settled to our satisfaction, descended again. Once more, an important section of the mountain had been conquered. On the evening of this same day, Wolfgang Nairz noted in his tape diary:

In the last few days Reinhold and Peter have reconnoitered with two Sherpas the camping site for our Camp III, a secure camping site in the middle of this roughly 45-degree- to 50-degree-steep flank. Today, Robert, the Bull, Horst, Franz and I also ascended with Sherpas in order to take equipment there, since for the next few days, from tomorrow onward, Peter and Reinhold will occupy this camp, and from there on will then belay the route to the South Col at an altitude of 26,000 feet.

It was warm; we felt well and, although tired, were not worn out. We sensed the thin air, but we didn't have

Two Sherpas on the Lhotse Face (at about 21,300 feet).

the feeling that we needed artificial oxygen, although we had already been working at an altitude at which others without oxygen equipment would get into great difficulties. Nevertheless, we didn't ascend, as planned, the next day, but decided to conserve our energy and rest for a while. So we remained in Camp II; it was April 13. Then Reinhold couldn't stand the inactivity any longer. With two Sherpas he pushed on up to over 25,000 feet. I, on the other hand, went down to the base camp, breaking a record in the process. I climbed down to the base camp in one hour and twenty minutes through the Valley of Silence and the icefall. For this stretch of about 6 miles you normally need four to five hours.

Reinhold, too, came back to the base camp later on the fifteenth of April, while Robert Schauer continued to work above with two Sherpas.

On the seventeenth of April, at Geneva Spur, he reached a height of 26,000 feet. The Geneva Spur is a mighty rib of rock that divides the Lhotse Face from the South Col. It was so named by a Swiss expedition in 1952. After Schauer had reached the Geneva Spur, the route to Camp IV was free, because from there on one can proceed on a relatively flat terrain over to the traverse leading to the South Col. Up to now everything had gone smoothly, perhaps too smoothly.

In fact, I had the feeling that it would not go so easily after this, and I was right, because on the seventeenth of April over the radio Hanns Schell reported stronger dislocations in the icefall. A crevasse had opened just as a couple of people were walking over it. Thank God, nothing had happened—at least, not yet.

On April 18, the Khumbu Icefall claimed its first victim. Over the radio Wolfgang Nairz announced to all camps: "Camp I and II, attention! An accident happened today in the Khumbu Icefall. The enormous platform where the Sherpas put down the double ladders has fallen in. A Sherpa happened to be at this spot at the time. He fell into the crevasse and can't be found. Please come in!"

From Camp II came the question: "And where are the other Sherpas? Are they down in the base camp, or are they still trying to recover the victim of the accident? Come in!"

Nairz replied: "Ang Phu was there with another Sherpa when Nuru fell in. They were about to fetch a ladder. However, the rope got in their way and they were not, therefore, roped together. Then it suddenly started to rumble, and the piece on which Nuru was standing caved in. Ang Phu is here; he says there was no chance at all of finding Nuru."

We were all deeply shaken, but, strangely enough, the Sherpas were not so sad as one would have assumed. Naturally they were upset, but after we had granted them a day of rest, they took up their work again without complaint.

The path through the Khumbu Glacier, which had been opened up by us, was covered in rubble. Robert Schauer who, from up above (that is to say, from Camp I), was organizing the belaying work and the possible recovery of the victim, reported over the radio from the site of the accident: "Over a length of about 650 feet the whole soil has subsided. The path led directly over the site of the accident. The breadth of the crevasse that has opened is sixty-five feet, but a rescue or recovery of Nuru is out of the question. The crevasse is covered from above with rubble through late falling ice."

9

I N MY DIARY I noted "Eighteenth and nineteenth of April—storm and heavy snowfall." The weather had worsened again. The belaying work was suspended, and the crews came home to the base camp exhausted. But on the twentieth of April, the storm abated; the sun broke through and it promised to be fine again.

Immediately after breakfast, I took Reinhold to one side: "What do you think? Shouldn't we make a first attempt?" "Why not?" was his reply. "After all, we've got the right to the first attack on the summit."

This right signified at the same time a certain obligation, since the rest of the team was naturally also intent on being able to go up. Any sign of hesitation on our part would hold up the whole operation. When we passed on our decision to the others, we met with unanimous agreement. The waiting period would, in any case, be shortened, because it was quite out of the question that two teams should start for the summit simultaneously. The reason for this was that it was necessary for the porters to transport equipment and oxygen cylinders up to the high-altitude camps for a second team. On the basis of experience, a two-man team had been able to cope best of all with an attack on the summit.

On the twenty-first of April we broke base camp and ascended to Camp I, accompanied by three Sherpas. We went at quite an easy pace and didn't overexert ourselves, so that we could adapt as well as possible to the altitude. In my diary I wrote: "From the base camp to Camp I about two hours," and, as a postscript: "I'm in very good shape."

On the next day we marched in a leisurely fashion to Camp II, and spent a very cold but peaceful night there. On April 23 we traversed the completely belayed Lhotse Face up to Camp III. I felt in excellent shape. By the evening I was hungry, and fetched a tin of sardines and ate them in one sitting. A little later I was overcome by a slight feeling of sickness combined with a feeling of pressure in the stomach. At first I ignored it and blamed the altitude for my condition. After all we were already on the other side of the 23,000-foot barrier.

My condition got worse and worse, cold sweat broke out, and spittle collected under my tongue. I just had to get out and be sick. I retched my guts out; my stomach and my throat burnt like fire. Obviously I was suffering from a genuine case of food poisoning. When I had nothing left to vomit but bitter bile, I crawled back into my sleeping bag, absolutely exhausted.

I knew that this time I just wouldn't be able to do it. Not this time and perhaps never. The altitude, the sickness, the pain, the loss of fluid and the effort of vomiting in themselves signified deadly danger. Without oxygen, going on in this condition would have been pure madness, and on top of everything the storm got up again toward morning.

"It's no good, Reinhold," I said. "I've probably upset my stomach with these tinned sardines, I just can't go on. You should turn back too. The weather is getting bad; there's going to be a storm. It's too dangerous."

I believe he was very disappointed, but he said nothing. He couldn't get to the summit on his own, but neither did he want to descend. For that reason he wanted to go up to the South Col and set up Camp IV there, at around 26,000 feet.

So he set off with two Sherpas. He had two tents with him, two gas stoves and a few gas cartridges, some other equipment and provisions. I felt absolutely wretched, but, because of the bad weather, I wanted to descend at all costs in order to wait for Reinhold in the advanced base camp. Our first attempt on the summit had failed and now it would be the turn of the others.

We were both within an inch of death when we separated that day.

The rising storm whirled up the snow and soon the three figures had disappeared from my view. I then set about my descent. With each step of the way I became weaker. Occasionally I leaned exhausted on my ice ax and rested for a few seconds before continuing along the yellow fixed ropes. I had the feeling that my strength simply wouldn't last out to the camp if I didn't hurry. Now fog came up, so dense that I could only find my bearings with difficulty once I had arrived at the foot of the Lhotse Face, where the fixed ropes ceased.

In the impenetrable windblown snow I became disoriented, and lost my sense of what was left and right. Certainly the lack of oxygen was playing its part in all this. For half an hour I wandered helplessly around and looked for the yellow marker flags, which we had pegged out. What finally helped me was my boundless will to survive, a will which once again instilled renewed strength within me. I eventually found one of the marker flags, and after about an hour, arrived at Camp II.

When I stumbled in alone, my comrades wore horrified looks. I must have looked terrible. And what had happened to Reinhold? I didn't know. But it was clear that he and the two Sherpas were struggling for their lives somewhere up there on the South Col.

As soon as I arrived in the camp, Wolfgang Nairz recorded what I had to report on tape. I spoke slowly and haltingly, somewhat confused, and with long pauses between each sentence. I was deeply discouraged and no longer believed in a victory over the summit.

"I am glad that I am in Camp II. During my whole mountaineering career I have never been as tired as I am today. I also don't know, is this Camp II . . . ? We climbed up very briskly yesterday. Reinhold went with me, but I must have done something wrong, I must have eaten something . . . sardines . . . or something like that. Within an hour it cleaned me out horribly. I vomited, nonstop, and it sapped so much of my strength that during the whole night I couldn't sleep a wink, although I had taken very powerful sleeping tablets. During the night I could not have slept for more than ten minutes. At first it was a little windy, but not so much that you could say it was bad. Because of this nasty business with my upset stomach I have naturally been held up a lot . . . but Reinhold went on early today with five Sherpas [in fact it was only two] into . . . up to the South Col. It was fantastically windy up there. The Sherpas have doubts as to whether they should pitch the tents at all. It will be difficult; it will be very, very difficult up there, without oxygen, at 27,000 feet. Up there, I think, all sorts of things can happen that you no longer have under your control. That's my personal belief, and I believe it will be extraordinarily difficult . . . I'm not so presumptuous as to say that it won't work out. . . . It must be warm. There mustn't be a storm under any circumstances. A storm like we have now. It will blow you out over the ridge. There you're simply . . . there you've no chance. I believe that since the 1920s, when it was tried a few times, nothing has changed very much. It's all still a matter of good luck. It depends on the weather and on the individual people whether you succeed or not. At the moment I am of the opinion that it will not succeed, but perhaps my poor condition is to blame for this. At the moment I see everything very pessimistically. If the sun shines and if there is no wind up there . . . , there are days when it is completely windless, then I believe that we can perhaps proceed from Camp IV . . . tried it. . . . The critical point lies certainly at 28,000 feet. If somebody still has the strength, and if somebody is prepared to gamble with the prospect of suffering severe damage, that's another question. . . . We will make another attempt, with Reinhold, if conditions are right, but under no circumstances will I push it so far that if I should get down I will end up an idiot. . . ."

That sounded to anybody who was listening like a renunciation of our grandiose plans. The message was relayed to the world and soon the news agencies announced: "Summit attempt on Mount Everest without oxygen fails."

As far as the rest of the world was concerned, we were at this moment nothing more than a couple of madmen, who had attempted something impossible and had ended up shipwrecked in the process.

The interest of the alpine climbing world now turned to the summit attempt of the rest of the team. Would, at least, an Austrian rope succeed for the first time in conquering Mount Everest, albeit with oxygen?

In the meantime there was no sign of life from Reinhold Messner. Was he even still alive?

10

O
N APRIL 27, an apparently ancient, bearded man
tottered into the base camp, followed by two
boys with faces like old men. It was Reinhold Messner
and his two Sherpas. Two fearful nights without oxygen
at over 26,000 feet had marked their faces. The Sherpas
were more dead than alive. Reinhold, whose every action
was slow and painful to watch, was still able at least to
report what had happened. He spoke incredibly slowly,
and his voice seemed to come from a remote distance.

They had penetrated the South Col up to the site
that had been planned for Camp IV. On the way the
storm had really attacked them. By making a great effort,
Reinhold and the two Sherpas had succeeded in putting
up a makeshift tent. But that was the limit of their
strength. The Sherpas were completely apathetic; they
thought they were going to die. Reinhold tried desperately to keep them awake, although he too was so tired
he could have dropped. But he, alone, knew that to fall
asleep would mean certain death from frostbite.

When the tent suddenly ripped with a loud noise in
a squall, their position was as good as hopeless. Nevertheless, Reinhold succeeded in patching up the tent pro-

visionally. He brewed tea and poured it into the Sherpas, who had crawled in panic into their sleeping bags, and no longer moved. He, too, drank as much of this hot tea as he possibly could. Their provisions had been limited, and would certainly not have sufficed for a longer stay. They also had no artificial oxygen with them.

Reinhold never mentioned if, as I had been during that stormy night in Camp II, he had been assailed by fears. But I believe that anybody who is fighting for his bare survival has no conception of worry or fear. What it means to survive a stormy night at such an altitude can only be imagined by somebody who has personally experienced it. Even under the most favorable circumstances every step at that altitude demands a colossal effort of will. You must force yourself to make every movement, reach for every handhold. You are perpetually threatened by a leaden, deadly fatigue. If you are exposed in such a situation to a storm, with squalls that reach a maximum speed of 81 miles per hour; if heavy windblown snow sets in, so thick that you can no longer see your hand in front of your face, your position becomes practically hopeless. You must cling on firmly to the ice in order not to be hurled off the mountain. Everybody is left to his own resources. If something happens to you, help is out of the question. Everybody has enough to do in trying to save himself.

Reinhold's achievement is all the more amazing in that he saved not only himself, but also his two Sherpas from certain death. He and his two companions spent two nights and one day in Camp IV. Reinhold spent most of the time in preventing the two Sherpas from going to sleep. He shouted at them, threatened them, insulted them and shook them awake constantly.

Recently I read that a Sherpa, who had not even taken part in this expedition, had declared at a press conference in Katmandu that Reinhold had maltreated a Sherpa. This was an allegation that caused great outrage among the audience. At first, this announcement simply amused me. I am convinced that Reinhold called down all the punishments of Hell on the two men; I would have done exactly the same in such a situation. It is necessary simply to prevent the people from going to sleep, or standing still during the descent. Only in this way could Reinhold save their lives.

I can remember at home in the Alps even slapping people around the ear if they wanted to give up, and later they actually thanked me. These attacks on Reinhold were, therefore, completely fabricated and unqualified. But they showed me once again that we mountaineers are only human beings, human beings with all the human weaknesses. Among us, too, you find a lot of jealousy, the kind that exists between actors. You encounter envy at other people's success, and sometimes, of course, business interests play a part in all this.

Where did things go from here? Reinhold was utterly exhausted. I was still in bad shape, although by the twenty-seventh of April I was already beginning to feel significantly better. I began to hatch new plans and wrote to my father-in-law:

Our summit attack, four days ago, failed due to a terrible storm, with a wind of around 81 miles per hour and temperatures of 49 degrees below zero Fahrenheit (measured on the South Col). Reinhold, who could no longer descend to Camp III where I found safety, spent two nights at 26,000 feet with a couple of Sherpas. Their tent was torn during the first night by the wind, and only with their last reserves of strength could they erect a second one. They had to stay awake for two nights holding on to the tent poles. At the end of all this, the Sherpas, and Messner too, were completely exhausted. Yesterday, after the storm had abated, they descended to the third and later to the second camp.

Now, Lois, rest assured that under no circumstances would I expose myself as far as this. I simply had the feeling on that day that the weather would turn nasty, and I was proved right. I shall do the same in the future. If conditions seem all right, okay, but if things look too dangerous, then I shall go back immediately. I shall try it once again with Messner, without oxygen, but if again it shouldn't succeed, I shall take two cylinders with me. I'm in better physical shape than Reinhold. I don't want to boast to you, but I would like you at home to feel reassured. We can protect ourselves well against the cold but the great danger is always the climb up through the Khumbu Icefall.

When you get this letter, we will be on our prospective second attack on the summit, and I hope that it comes off. Now in May it is getting noticeably "warmer." Instead of minus 49°, it is about 10° less at 26,000 feet, and the weather is also stabilizing itself before the beginning of the monsoon (end of May).

Lois, that in brief was our situation report, rest assured (for the second time!) that I am keeping up my courage, that I am taking no unnecessary risks, and that I hope to be back home with you in two to three weeks.

As always when I needed to cheer myself up psychologically, I went through the old written accounts of the first attempts to conquer the highest summit in the world. It was not until 1852 that it was discovered that the mountain at the frontier between Tibet and Nepal, which had previously been designated with the Roman numeral IV, was the highest mountain in the world. Moreover, it was found that this mountain, which must have consisted of geologically recent rock, grew every ten years by a further yard, since this mountain range like the Alps is still in the process of evolving. The natives called the mountain "Chomolungma," which means "Mother over the Gods of the Country." Its present name comes from the British geographer Sir George Everest. In the middle of the nineteenth century, commissioned by the English Viceroy of India, he undertook a land-surveying project in the Himalayan region and performed distinguished services in so doing.

But it wasn't until 1921 that Sir Charles Bell obtained from the Dalai Lama, the Chief of State of the then priest state of Tibet, the authorization to enter the forbidden land, and to undertake a reconnaissance expedition to Everest. This expedition, under their leader, Lieutenant Colonel C. K. Howard Bury, climbed the mountain from its north side and reached an altitude of about 23,000 feet without using oxygen equipment, which at that time was quite unheard of in mountaineering. One member of the expedition, George Leigh Mallory, wrote after his return:

Above all you've got to have luck; one moment of benevolent humour which temporarily at least pacifies the cruel nature of Mount Everest. Let us not forget that a cold severity dwells in

THE COLOR ILLUSTRATIONS

1. Peter Habeler at the summit of the Hidden Peak (26,500 feet).
2. Peter Habeler after his return from Mount Everest.
3. The Dhaulāgiri (27,000 feet) with the South Wall.
4. A giant avalanche on the Dhaulāgiri South Wall.
5. The Ama Dablam (22,400 feet) in the Khumbu Himal.
6. Mount Everest (29,000 feet) left, and the Lhotse (28,000 feet) right, seen from Thyangboche.
7. New snow at the base camp at an altitude of 17,400 feet.
8. The beginning of the Khumbu Icefall.
9. The Nuptse (26,000 feet) seen from the base camp.
10. Kitchen tent and operations table at base camp. Right, Nairz, Knoll, Oppurg and Ölz; left, Bergmann.
11. Oppurg, Knoll and Schauer on the ascent through the Khumbu Icefall.
12. In the Khumbu Icefall.
13. Ascent through the Khumbu Icefall.
14. The glacier crevasses in the Khumbu Icefall are bridged by means of aluminum ladders.
15. Camp I, altitude 19,000 feet. Left to right: Eric Jones of HTV (British television company), the Sherpa Tati, and Peter Habeler.
17. West Cwm, the Valley of Silence, altitude 20,000 feet.
16. The first attack on the Khumbu Icefall.
18. Penetration of the Lhotse flank. In the background is the South-west Wall of Everest.
19. Mount Everest (29,000 feet).
20. Peter Habeler at Camp III, altitude 23,600 feet. In the background is Eric Jones.
21. Ascent from Camp III to Camp IV by means of the yellow rope, at altitude of 24,600 feet.
22. Peter Habeler by the Chinese surveying tripod on the summit of Mount Everest.
23. Peter Habeler at the South Col (altitude 26,000 feet) after his return from the summit.

3 △   4 ▽

△ 9 10 ▽

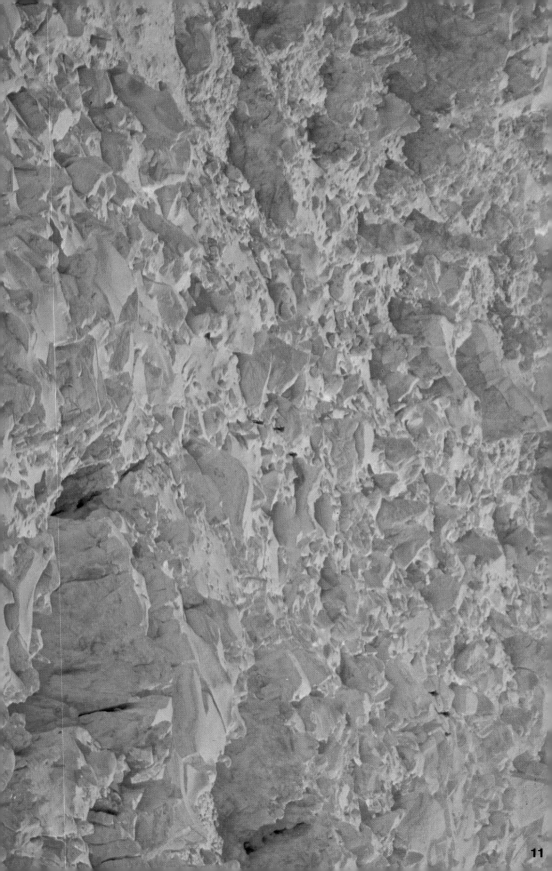

15 △   16 ▽

17 △   18 ▽

this highest of all mountains, a severity so fearful and so murderous that if you have any sense you would do well to hesitate on the threshold of your ultimate goal and tremble.

But only a year later, on the tenth of May 1922, Mallory made another attempt on Everest. The irresistible urge to ascend to the summit had taken hold of him. Without oxygen, he reached an altitude of about 26,000 feet, but then had to turn back again because of bad weather. Later, he fell with his companions in an avalanche and was lucky to survive, while seven of his Sherpas were killed.

Then he tried a third time. On June 7, 1924, he ascended with his friend Andrew Irvine, at six o'clock in the morning from Camp VI, which was established at a height of 26,400 feet. A couple of hours later they were sighted for the last time by a member of the expedition, N. E. Odell, at an altitude of about 28,000 feet. At that time they were on the northeast ridge and were moving slowly forward. Suddenly they disappeared in fog and were never seen again.

After this accident, access to Everest was barred to foreigners for nine years, and Nepal refused also to authorize any attempts on the mountain from the south side.

Yet in 1933, it was again English mountaineers who set off for Everest. Their leader was Hugh Ruttledge. The men set up their Camp VI at 26,900 feet, that is well below the place at which Mallory and Irvine were last seen. A snowstorm forced them to turn back, and on their return journey they found Mallory's ice ax. This could perhaps indicate that Mallory was already on his way back when he was killed, and one could possibly conclude from this that he had previously reached the summit. This was indeed a breathtaking thought: men in knickerbockers and hobnailed boots with inadequate equipment on top of Everest!

The more I read about the exploits of these tough characters from the 1920s, the more confident I became that our venture would succeed.

In 1934 an eccentric individualist attempted to conquer the summit. This was the Yoga devotee Maurice Wilson. He was convinced that he could establish direct contact between the soul and his body if he fasted for three weeks. Then, he believed, it would be possible for him to reach the summit of Everest. First of all he planned to fly up as high as possible in a plane, and make a crash landing, so that he would then be able to go up the rest of the mountain without too much effort. But, unfortunately, during an intermediate landing, his plane was confiscated. He bribed some Sherpas who smuggled him over the border and, equipped with only rice water, warm clothes and an ice ax, he climbed up to Camp III. In 1960 a Chinese expedition, which had ascended from the Tibet side, found his corpse and recorded this gruesome find on film. The film was later shown in Europe.

In 1935, 1936, and 1938, three more expeditions failed due to bad weather. Then the war broke out, and all attempts to conquer the hitherto unconquered mountain were suspended. It was not until 1947 that another individualist, a Canadian called Earl C. Denman, tried again. In contrast to the unhappy Wilson, he had some knowledge of mountaineering. He too crossed the border illegally, disguised as a lama, and took two Sherpas with him. One of them was Tenzing Norgay, the man who, six years later in 1953, was to reach the summit with Edmund Hillary.

Denman and the two Sherpas had ideal weather conditions and reached the south flank of Everest. But then the Sherpas refused to go on any farther; they considered Denman's equipment to be too scanty. He, therefore, continued alone and reached an altitude of 21,600 feet before being forced to turn back. He recorded his experiences in the book *Alone on Everest,* and its sales earned him a great deal of money.

And then in 1951 a British expedition, in which Hillary took part, discovered a promising route to the summit. For the first time, Nepal had issued the authorization to explore Everest from the south. Throughout previous years, climbers had traditionally ascended to the Everest massif from Tibet on the north side. However, in the meantime, Tibet had become a Chinese province, and therefore this route was barred to Western expeditions. The expedition under Eric Shipton discovered the route via the icefall into the Valley of Silence, via the Lhotse Face and the South Col, and then on over the South Summit to the main summit. Shipton did not, however, go up himself, but postponed the attack on the summit until later. On the way back, he and his companions discovered the track of the *yeti,* the mysterious Abominable Snowman, and took photos of its footprints. In the process a legend was born, which has preoccupied even serious scientists right up to the present day.

In the meantime oxygen technology had been much

improved. The cylinders had become smaller and easier to handle. Masks, one-way valves and closed-circuit systems had been developed through which oxygen could no longer escape. The rest of the equipment now also weighed considerably less. Climbers started using man-made fibers and lightweight down equipment.

One Swiss expedition had almost reached the summit in 1952. Again the Sherpa Tenzing was with them. Raymond Lambert, Flory, Aubert and Tenzing reached the last camp on May 27. On the twenty-eighth of May 1952, Tenzing and Lambert set off. They reached a height of 27,765 feet. But then their strength deserted them. Suffering from altitude sickness and great exhaustion, they had to give up. On the twenty-ninth of May they returned to Camp V, completely spent.

A little later a second team started. One of the participants later wrote:

Our breath became shorter and shorter the higher we got. We kept on pausing in the hope that our physical strength would return, but that was an illusion. At this altitude men cannot regenerate themselves anymore. On the contrary, every minute which passes eats up your physical energy. Even the strongest man is weakened.

The second team came within 787 feet of the summit and then they, too, had to give up. Raymond Lambert noted:

Every Everest expedition learns something new as to how this mountain may finally be conquered. Every expedition clambers up, as it were, on the shoulders of the previous one. Our expedition taught us a clear lesson. We now know that the best age for Everest climbers is between thirty and forty. We know the advantages of acclimatization and we have discovered at what distances from each other the camps are best set up.

This was certainly a step forward, but in the post-monsoon period of the same year, a second expedition consisting of the same men failed, owing to a series of accidents and bad weather conditions. On returning to the base camp, two Sherpas died of overexertion, and another Sherpa was killed in the icefall. Three others suffered fractures, and then on top of everything else, a storm broke. Despite this, Tenzing, Lambert, Reiss and seven Sherpas climbed far up until the storm finally forced them to retrace their steps.

The attempt by the Russians to be the first to climb the mountain also ended in tragedy. They tried it at the beginning of the winter of 1952. Thirty-five experienced mountaineers, among them well-known altitude phys-iologists and medical men, arrived via Tibet at the North Face of the mountain. The expenditure was colossal. Five army planes transported the equipment from Moscow, via Novosibirsk and Irkutsk to Lhasa, but the approach march to the base camp took longer than expected. The team had a portable radio set with them and were in direct contact with Moscow. Six men set off to the sum-mit, taking the radio set with them. They transmitted over the radio the fact that they had occupied a camp at an altitude of 26,410 feet and that, if the weather held, they would undertake an attempt on the summit in about two days. Then the radio went dead. Moscow sounded the alarm.

Search parties ascended and deployed, but the six

mountaineers remained lost. After eighteen days the search was provisionally abandoned because winter was setting in.

In the following year the search was continued, again without success. It was assumed that the summit team had been overrun by an avalanche and dragged down to the valley.

Officially, nobody ever heard anything about this expedition, but a few facts trickled through. For example, the fact that the equipment was supposed to have been inadequate and out of date. Later, those responsible for this over-hasty and inadequately organized venture were called to account and severely punished.

The first conquest of Everest succeeded at last in 1953. Hillary and Tenzing began their historic ascent on the twenty-ninth of May. The day before, five of them had penetrated via the South Col to a height of 27,500 feet. The mountaineers Lowe and Gregory and the second Sherpa functioned as a support and supply team, while Hillary and Tenzing were to make the decisive attack on the summit.

On that morning at four o'clock they crawled out of their tents and set off on the route, while the three others returned to the South Col. Hillary and Tenzing were confronted by colossal, overhanging snow cornices. Every step was highly dangerous. Climbing over the southeast ridge, they arrived at a point not far below the South Summit where they rested. The first of the two oxygen cylinders brought by each man was empty. They had now only one cylinder each with which to complete their journey. Would that be enough? Hillary made feverish

Sir Edmund Hillary, first conqueror of Mount Everest.

calculations. Two hundred eleven gallons of oxygen at a
flow of .8 gallons per minute. He calculated that that
would suffice for four-and-a-half hours. That was all the
time they had to get up and then back again to the last
camp, where the reserve cylinders were stored.

The decisive barrier before the summit was an
eighty-two-foot-high rock step, as smooth as glass and

almost without foot- or handholds. This was later called the Hillary Step. To the east side of the rock step clung an enormous snowdrift. Here they decided to ascend. Hillary went first on the rope, while Tenzing did the belaying work on the firm footing. He went up inch by inch, always expecting the cornice to cave in. Using his knees, shoulders and arms, Hillary levered his way up, until he reached firm ground above and sank down exhausted. Then Tenzing followed him by the same route, this time Hillary belaying. Having arrived at the top, Tenzing fell spreadeagled like a dead bird in the snow.

They went higher and higher up the ridge. The original verve with which they had started that day had left them. The minutes slipped past, and they still hadn't reached their goal. In the meantime they were engaged in a genuine race against time—their oxygen supply was rapidly coming to an end.

Suddenly, Hillary realized that he couldn't go up any more but only down—he was standing on the highest peak on earth! Tenzing grinned. The delighted look on his face was very much apparent, in spite of his oxygen mask, upon which long icicles were hanging. Then the two men, so unequal in size, embraced each other and clapped each other on the back for minutes on end until they ran out of breath.

For the first time in history, Everest had been conquered; for the first time ever an Everest expedition had attained its goal.

But the many unsuccessful expeditions before had not been in vain. Every one of these expeditions had played its role in the history of the conquest of Everest because, as Raymond Lambert had already said, each new expedition was able to put to good use the lessons learned from previous ones. These memoirs were particularly useful to me, as Hillary and Tenzing's main problem was that they did not know whether what they were attempting was humanly possible. In this respect Reinhold and I found ourselves in a comparable situation; we too were risking a step into the unknown.

I knew from my research that it was possible to penetrate extreme altitudes without oxygen—and still survive. After all, following Hillary's conquest of the peak using oxygen, the first ascent without oxygen was the next logical step.

In reflecting upon these past achievements my spiritual equilibrium returned. My stomach pains subsided and my confidence grew.

In the meantime Reinhold, too, became more cheerful. After a couple of days we agreed that we would attempt the summit once again, after the first oxygen team had made their assault.

11

NAIRZ, Bergmann, Schauer and Ang Phu were in top physical condition. It was for this reason that they were chosen to form the next summit team. For their ascent they would follow exactly the same route as Hillary and Tenzing had taken when they first conquered the mountain. Leaving Camp IV on the South Col, they planned to stop at one intermediate camp, our Camp V, in order to arrive via the southeast ridge at the South Summit, and finally at the main summit. Twelve Sherpas were to accompany them as a support team. At this point I should like to allow Wolfgang Nairz to speak for himself.

"Now it was a case of thinking clearly and coolly. At the South Col we had calculated exactly what we would need in the way of oxygen. We knew that in Camp V, that is to say in the last camp of the ascent, the four of us would need at least another sixteen cylinders, one for each of us to sleep, two for ascending, and finally one for the return journey to the South Col. These sixteen cylinders had been carried up for us by our Sherpas. The next morning, however, we were shocked to discover that during the night, our Sherpas had used up three of the cylinders which we would need for the summit. Now we had to act quickly. We checked through all the cylinders that were lying around from earlier expeditions to the top, and found among them a few American ones, which were still half full. Our technical genius, Horst Bergmann, skillfully adapted our French breathing masks to these American cylinders. Equipped with this reserve we set off again, each of us carrying fifty-five pounds of gear on our backs.

"We made a track up a steep trench, and in the afternoon cleared the site for Camp V. We pitched our tents, brewed tea, and then crawled into our sleeping bags. At this point our assault on the summit very nearly came to grief. While replenishing a gas stove, the gas suddenly streamed into the tent. It exploded, and in a flash the whole tent was in flames. Horst, who had kept his oxygen mask on, was able, however, to extinguish the flames quickly.

"It was pretty stormy during the night and it also snowed again. On the next day, at five in the morning, we began to cook, and at ten minutes past eight we were ready to set off. Horst and I went first, initially up to our knees in snow, then later the snow reached to our stomachs. Shortly below the South Summit, Horst discovered that his oxygen cylinder was almost empty. His apparatus had registered an apparent oxygen surplus and he had consequently used up too much. We waited for Robert and Ang Phu. During the ascent, Robert had used up less oxygen, and offered Horst his reserve cylinder. After this, Robert and Ang Phu climbed on ahead, while Horst and I remained at the South Summit in order to film the progress of our two friends. They arrived at the Hillary Step, a precipitous rock step of a ridgelike course. Robert mastered it magnificently and then he disappeared from our view. We followed him, hardly speaking at all but communicating only by hand signals.

"When we reappeared behind a knoll we suddenly saw Robert and Ang Phu. They had reached the summit and were standing next to a three-legged surveying instrument, left there by the Chinese during their conquest of the summit in 1975. The two waved down to us. Horst continued to film the last few feet, while we slowly climbed. When we got up there, we fell on each other's necks. Ang Phu even kissed my feet and said again and again: *"Para Sahib, Para Sahib!"* (Chief of the Expedition, Chief of the Expedition!) The wind had dropped completely, we unbuckled our rucksacks, stood on the summit, looked around and marveled and photographed."

This was on the third of May 1978. The expedition had accomplished its initial goal—the first conquest of the summit by an Austrian team. Naturally, Nairz's ambition was to get as many members of the team as possible to the summit, but he hadn't reckoned with Ang Phu. After the *sirdar* had reached the summit, he felt that he had attained his own personal expeditionary goal. When he got down to the base camp again, therefore, he seemed to lack the necessary stimulus to motivate his Sherpas as before, and to drive them on. We had the distinct impression that the efforts of the Sherpas had slack-

Franz Oppurg at the South Col with oxygen cylinder and breathing ▷ apparatus.

ened markedly. They pointed to their thighs and signified that they would need at least two weeks to regain fitness.

It is true that they had given of their all during the ascent of the first team. Fifteen of them had been involved in dragging heavy loads and oxygen cylinders up to the South Col. In doing this, each of them had carried at least forty pounds. Now all the urgency and drive had gone out of the Sherpa chief, and thus his people too changed into a lower gear. They got up later in the mornings, and climbed more slowly through the icefall, each of them very much aware of just how dangerous it was, since one of their members had been killed here.

Ang Phu directed the porters from the base camp by assembling the loads together. But he did not go up again. The Sherpas were unable to understand why all the members of the expedition wanted to make it to the summit. For them the whole affair was practically at an end since a team, including the leader of the expedition, had reached the summit. This particularly affected the three-man rope of Dr. Margreiter, Helmut Hagner and Hanns Schell. Most of the porters refused to drag oxygen to the South Col once again, so the three tried going it alone. They carried some of their cylinders themselves, but were then forced to give up. The reasons for this were, first, because the weather wasn't good enough and, second, because Hanns Schell went down with a severe cold. The failure of this team caused a lot of bad feeling in the camp. Wolfgang Nairz was reproached for having the wrong Sherpa accompany him to the summit. In my opinion this was completely unjustifiable.

I was very sorry about the whole incident. I knew

that Dr. Margreiter and Helmut Hagner had prepared themselves particularly well for this expedition, and I also knew that they had contributed a great deal in getting the expedition off the ground at all.

This quarrel, however, did not directly affect Reinhold and myself very much. We constituted a rather special team, and in any case we scarcely needed any Sherpas for our attempt without oxygen. We only wanted to take two porters with us, who would carry our gear up to the South Col.

Our next attempt on the summit was imminent. In normal circumstances, one team, whose first assault on the summit has failed, must wait until the remaining teams have had their turn before trying again. But from the very start it had been agreed that we would be treated differently. We had paid more money into the kitty than the others, and we were therefore entitled to greater freedom of movement and decision. Without this, we wouldn't have been able to carry out what we had planned. For this very reason the go-slow of the Sherpas affected us least of all.

We remained in the base camp until the first of May, passing the time in a leisurely fashion, and ended up in better form than we had been during the entire previous expedition. I believe that it was only at this point that I was really well acclimatized. This was also true of Reinhold, who literally prospered visibly from hour to hour. The weather was magnificent and it was clear to both of us that it was now or never!

On the second of May we prepared ourselves once again for storming the summit. This time we just had to succeed. If we failed again, we wouldn't possess either the mental or the physical power to attempt the assault a third time.

On this occasion, we were very cautious in our predictions when departing from the base camp. We never asserted: "We will conquer Everest without oxygen." We said at most: "We want to attempt it." This, in Reinhold's case, amounted to saying: "I will attempt it in any case. Right up to the limit of what is possible." On one point we were absolutely determined, and stressed it again and again: "In no event will we go up Everest using oxygen. If it is not possible without an oxygen mask we will turn back; we will give up."

That was our philosophy, and we had committed ourselves to it once and for all. At home in our native Tyrol, during preliminary discussions with expedition participants and journalists, it had been easy to say this. It sounds good and one is proud of one's own attitude. But when you are up on the mountain, things look different. You don't admit it, and you never speak to anybody about it, but up here, with the shining pyramid of this king of mountains before your eyes, you are seized with summit fever.

Already in the base camp, there were days when I thought secretly to myself: I would like to get up there —at any cost—to stand up there and look down on Tibet, and on the other mountain giants far below me. And then my conscience would take over. Would you really, in spite of everything that you have said, bring yourself to go up with breathing equipment, if necessary? My pride would not allow it. I felt bound by my word. Voices quarreled within me, and it really brought home to me the meaning of the saying: Everybody is divided within himself.

Now on the morning of the second of May, this conflict within me was forgotten, or perhaps I should say suppressed. We climbed up at a good speed, bypassed Camp I and headed immediately for Camp II. It was very hot that day. Inside the tent, the temperature was over 108 degrees Fahrenheit. There was not a breath of air. Even on the summit there was no wind. This would favor victory for Nairz's team.

In Camp II we then heard over the radio the announcement of Nairz's success. Cracking voices shouted into the microphone and we shouted back, absolutely overjoyed for them. Not only were we pleased for them, but also for ourselves, since the ideal weather conditions promised success for us too.

Reinhold had once admitted: "I undertake an expedition for myself alone, and for nobody else." He was being honest. On thinking it over, this could also be said to a certain extent of myself. I needed this success for quite personal reasons, just as much as Reinhold did.

Any sort of romantic idealism would be pure hypocrisy. I wanted to do something that nobody thought possible: something that I would be able to keep for myself alone. I cannot really answer, in simple terms, the question: "Why do you climb mountains at all?" If one wants to prove oneself, there are other ways in which to do it. A mountaineer has no spectators and no applause, and if he achieves something extraordinary, there are always doubters and enviers: "Why do you do it then?" Does it sound too sentimental if I say that mountains are in my blood? Mountains enticed me for as long as I can remember. Even as a six- or seven-year-old, I sought out the biggest clumps of rock around Mayrhofen in order to practice my climbing. I got through a terrifyingly large amount of iodine and adhesive tape at home! The older I became, the more daring the climbing excursions I undertook. My friends had long since given up trying to emulate me, and while they played football down in the valley, or taught each other the noble art of card playing, I was up on the glaciers of the Zillertal armed with my grandfather's ice ax.

All mountaineers knew me as the lunatic boy who tackled the most difficult glacier tours solo. To salve their consciences a little they warned me of the many dangers connected with the ice, and how important it was to exercise caution. I learned how to recognize a longitudinal crevasse and how to skirt a lateral crevasse. With an ice ax that reached up to my armpit, and a rucksack half as large as myself, I had soon attained the summits of all the 9000-foot mountains that I could reach from my house over the weekend. If on Monday mornings, often frozen through and exhausted, I turned up late for my classes, then my teachers benevolently turned a blind eye. Only my mother regarded my passion for mountaineering with displeasure, and did all in her power to keep me away from the mountains—but to no avail.

At the age of fourteen I left my modern secondary school in Mayrhofen and I went to the School of Commerce at Vorarlberg. Naturally, I was now going to attempt the summits there. At seventeen, I was fortunate enough to meet experienced mountaineers who were willing to train this largely self-taught youth to become a professional mountaineer. This was not just to benefit me, but also because they felt I could be useful to them. Small and agile though I was, and in fact have remained, I was excellently suited for the role of an advance climber. Using all of my strength and skill, I was able to guide my comrades through the most difficult traverses. In this way I graduated in the best mountaineering school imaginable.

It is true that under no circumstances did my mother want me to become a professional mountaineer. So to please her, I trained for the trade of glass painter. I attended a technical school for four years and at the end of the course took my final examination. In the meantime, however, I was drawn again and again to the mountains. Sometimes I was employed as a mountain guide, and in the winter holidays, in order to earn extra money, I worked in the ski school and also undertook extended winter tours with visitors. The older I became, the more difficult were my mountaineering expeditions, but no serious accidents ever occurred. Naturally, I developed a pronounced routine. My movements on the mountain were now so much a part of my flesh and blood that my actions became pure reflexes. I climbed with almost automatic sureness of touch, and I also started training to increase my speed. This was most important to my method of climbing. I often wondered why other mountaineers stayed for three or four days on a wall, and bivouacked at sites that were constantly exposed to rockfall.

The Yerupaja Grande (21,800 feet) in the Andes. On the Austrian-Andes expedition in 1969, the West Alpine style was, for the first time, applied outside Europe.

I, on the other hand, made it a principle to climb up a wall as quickly as possible and then down again, so as not to have to camp out for the night.

In time I began climbing the Alps, where I made difficult ice tours. Among other things, I conquered the Freney-Pillar on Mont Blanc in 1966, the second traversing, in an astonishingly rapid time. The Walker Pillar in the Grandes Jorasses in France became one of the first really big climbing jobs I undertook with Reinhold Messner, with whom I was then already an intimate friend. It turned out that we shared a common interest in the mountains. But at that time I was still doing many solo climbs.

In 1969 I took part in the Tyrolean Andes expedition during which we climbed the Yerupaja. In 1970 Karl Herrligkoffer offered to take me with him on his Nānga Parbat expedition. Reinhold, too, was invited. At first I agreed, but then an opportunity presented itself for me to spend the winter as a ski instructor in the U.S.A. So again I had to put aside thoughts of the Himalayas, which had enticed me for so long. The place reserved for me was taken by Reinhold's brother, Günter; on that trip he was killed in an ice avalanche.

The Americans detained me for a while. In order to compensate myself for the lost Nānga Parbat opportunity, in 1970 I went with a couple of American mountaineers to California, into the Yosemite valley near San Francisco. The south wall of El Capitan was considered then, and still is, to be one of the most difficult walls in the world. I was the first European to conquer it.

In 1974 Reinhold and I conquered the Eiger North

Face in record time. Our achievement attracted international interest. And then in 1975 I went to the Himalayas for the first time. In the meantime, I had been a professional alpine guide for ten years. Again I went with Reinhold. Our two-man expedition to the Hidden Peak caused a furor at that time in the professional world. Nobody had ever thought it possible to attack a 26,000-foot mountain with only a two-man team, let alone to conquer it.

In the autumn of 1975 I married Regina, a girl from my native Mayrhofen, whom I had known for several years. When we left for the Dhaulāgiri, Regina was three months pregnant, but she had kept this to herself. She didn't want me to give up the Dhaulāgiri expedition, on which I had already set my heart.

The Dhaulāgiri South Wall, which we were unsuccessful in climbing in 1977, was a preparatory expedition for the Everest trip. Without our Dhaulāgiri experience, where each day we encountered avalanches that thundered down the wall face, we would have found Everest much harder. Seen in this light, Mount Everest without oxygen was for me the logical culmination of my whole previous mountaineering career, the natural and inevitable crowning touch to everything that I had previously achieved.

We waited in Camp II until Nairz, Schauer and Berg-

Pages 151–155
Peter Habeler ascending the southwest face of El Capitan in California. El Capitan is considered to be one of the most difficult free-climbing faces in the world.

mann arrived from the summit, since I was very anxious to have a few words with Robert Schauer. Before his ascent he had assured me: "I am going to go as far without oxygen as is humanly possible; in any case at least up to 26,000 feet."

Schauer was ambitious, and I could most easily imagine that it would be he who would achieve the ascent of the summit without oxygen. Perhaps he still lacked the mountaineering experience, the automatic sureness of touch of Reinhold and myself, which enabled us to find hand- and footholds without even thinking. For the two of us, climbing had long since become a mere reflex. But Robert Schauer certainly had no doubts about his abilities, and just like us he had at his disposal important qualities that make every great mountaineering success possible: he was tough and he had endurance, and he excelled in critical situations.

When Robert finally arrived in Camp II with Nairz, he said: "Listen, it couldn't be done. From Camp IV on I had to put on my mask; on the way I took it off a couple of times, but after a few steps I had the feeling that I was suffocating. I became incredibly tired."

This was a bad blow for me.

"Impossible," Nairz confirmed to us as well. "You'll never be able to move fast enough to succeed."

Once again I was plagued with doubts, but this time more violently than ever before. From minute to minute I changed my mind. Should I go? Should I give up? I couldn't answer, but Robert, in contrast to the others, had not after all said: "You will not succeed," he had only said: "*I* haven't succeeded."

Later, it is true, he admitted to me: "I no longer believed that you could succeed." Today it is clear to me why he was unable to continue without oxygen once he had taken off his mask. With a sudden deoxygenation, much more serious effects set in than if one has ascended slowly and has thus acclimatized oneself to the oxygen starvation. There may also be a psychological factor at work here. As long as the equipment and mask are at hand, the temptation to use oxygen is overpowering. At no time is it a matter of life and death, because you've only got to move your hand and once again you're attached to the life-giving gas. This is a sort of reassurance, and therefore you don't strive to use the hidden reserves that are within us all. There is one other factor as well. An oxygen cylinder, when full, weighs almost fifteen-and-a-half pounds; that's an extra load to carry, and one with which a climber can only cope if oxygen is actually being inhaled.

After the conversation with Schauer, I crept quietly into my tent. I had brought my photographs of Regina and my son with me from the base camp. I put them down in front of me and held a mute conversation with them. I didn't really feel any fear of death. My anxiety revolved much more around my mental and physical health. If I was to lose my mind, or my toes and fingers through frostbite, as had happened to Maurice Herzog during the first ascent of Annapurna, then I would no longer be able to continue with my career as an alpine guide. My future, and that of my family, would be destroyed. And what if I gave up now, ignominiously disappeared and returned home? Regina had said to me on my departure: "The greatest success for me is if you come home safe and well."

Perhaps it would really have shown greater bravery if I had turned back, for the sake of my family, and thus exposed myself to the ridicule of the public. I didn't know. With the best will in the world, I couldn't decide. And what would Reinhold, my partner, say? Could I do that to him? After all, he was relying on me; he would probably not be able to find a second man to go with him, and would therefore have to give up as well. Yet of one thing I was quite certain: Reinhold would understand my decision, whatever it might be, and accept it willingly, without questioning me further about it. It would not have affected our friendship.

Anyway, I could ask him myself, and I did: "Reinhold, what would you do if I were to give up?" He looked at me long and seriously and then replied: "Consider well what you are doing. I can't make up your mind for you. In any case, I am going to attempt the ascent. I would not like to say that I would have nothing to lose, but nevertheless I should like to make the attempt."

There was neither disappointment nor scorn in his voice; he simply said exactly what he was thinking. But at the same time he knew that I would never leave him in the lurch; he knew me well enough after all these years.

Only to myself were things not yet clear. Finally, I had an idea. I went to the radio set, called the base camp and demanded to speak to Bull.

"Bull, I have thought it over," I said, "I'm not going to go up, after all, without oxygen. But I do want to go up, and what's more I would like the two of us to go up together as a two-man rope. Come up, and we will try it."

At that moment I didn't care a damn what Reinhold was thinking or doing. Bull agreed at first, but he must have then talked it over with the two other members of his three-man team, Franz Oppurg and Josl Knoll, to whom he had been assigned for an attack on the summit. The radio conversations went back and forth for a while. In the meantime, Nairz had descended with his team back to the base camp. Finally, the Bull declined: "Peter, I'd really like to go up with you, and I'd be ready to do so at any time. It would be the most marvelous thing for me, but I just cannot do this to Oppurg and Knoll. Out."

He wasn't coming with me, and I wouldn't find any other rope mate. In fact the Bull did later make the ascent, not with Knoll and Oppurg, but with Reinhard Karl.

I discovered what was really going on at the base camp shortly afterward through a radio conversation with Nairz, who had tuned in meanwhile as mediator. After my question to Bull, there had been a tremendous uproar. Oppurg and Knoll, especially, did not hold back the harsh words: "That Habeler, smart aleck, first of all he trumpets to the whole world that he is going to go up without oxygen, and then he backs down without even trying it."

I felt very hurt; from these two especially I hadn't expected such a harsh reaction. I was gripped by a burning anger. For me, the question as to whether I was going to go up with or without oxygen was now settled. I wanted to go up with Reinhold as planned, just to prove myself to the others. And all my other reservations were completely swept away. I didn't care a damn either about the possible physical or mental damage that might result. I was governed only by a blind anger that drove me on.

In mountaineering, anger is not by any means a rare driving force. Hermann Buhl, for example, attacked the summit of the Nānga Parbat out of anger, because he knew that the lower camps had already been dismantled, and that he had no secure return path to follow. Also Anderl Heckmair, the first conqueror of the Eiger North Face, had once told me that in 1938, he had twice fallen from a particularly difficult traverse. Suddenly, he had been seized by such a burning anger, that in one single go he had clambered over the difficult iced-up section, and had thereby conquered the wall. I had had similar experiences. Whenever it seemed that I just couldn't go on because a wall was too difficult, and when I thought that I had finally reached the limits of my strength, I would get so angry that I would finally clamber up like a weasel.

To Reinhold, I simply said: "I'm going with you." And he replied: "Great, let's try it tomorrow. We'll climb up nice and slowly to Camp III. Eric Jones would like to come too since he wants to film us. We'll take two Sherpas. They can carry some of our equipment, and perhaps help us on the way from Camp III to Camp IV by tracking through the snow."

On May 6 we climbed in four hours up to Camp III. The route was long and steep, but we knew it already. We walked quite loosely, and I banished all doubts from my mind. Somehow, I thought, we are going to do it.

The route to Camp III had always been something of

a touchstone. Again and again I had observed how our comrades had had to fight like mad to get up the steep Lhotse Face without oxygen. But if they had attached the oxygen cylinders in Camp III, they progressed much more easily. This interesting experience was a good criterion for our own performance. It had only taken us four hours for the ascent, and none of the others came anywhere near to competing with this. Eric Jones, who went with us, had taken eight hours. This was a good omen. We sensed that this time we were going to be lucky. We drank soup and vast quantities of tea. We drank it in order, as it were, to build up supplies within our bodies, because the farther we ascended the more difficult it would be to melt sufficient snow on the tiny stoves. Other than this, there was scarcely anything more to do or say. It was now only a question of getting as much sleep as possible. Reinhold and I had both taken our sleeping tablets with us. Reinhold took his usual Mogadon, and I my customary Valium. At great altitudes, one is so on edge because of the unaccustomed climatic conditions and the exertions of the ascent that it is impossible to get to sleep without sleeping tablets.

Sometime during the night I woke up. It was cold and somewhat stormy, the walls of the tent shook, and from afar I heard the thunder of falling avalanches.

Together with Eric Jones, we left Camp III very early in the morning of May 7, and set off on the difficult ascent via the South Col to Camp IV. The sun was shining down from a cloudless sky and we still felt fresh and strong. The wind during the night had swept the snow into high drifts, and we had to make a track while covered up to our hips in the snow. Our favorite Sherpa, Tati, assisted us. Eric Jones soon fell behind, because with his camera he couldn't move forward nearly so fast as we could. However, gradually we too began to slacken our pace as a result of the altitude. No wonder either, because we had now crossed the 26,000-foot barrier.

Fatigue crept into our bones and made them seem as heavy as lead. Our breathing came in short and shallow bursts, and we didn't seem to be making any progress at all. But after four hours' climbing, and feeling very exhausted, the South Col camp finally came into view. While we waited for Eric, we brewed up some tea. But Eric didn't appear. Either he was taking much longer than we would have thought necessary, or he had simply turned back. Two hours went past, then three, and still there was no sign of him. We became really worried. After all, like us, he was making the attempt without oxygen. We hoped that he hadn't collapsed.

However, Eric is 100 percent an Englishman, and on the dot of five o'clock—teatime—he appeared, dropped down exhausted and gasped: "Tea, please!" He had taken eight-and-a-half hours to cover this stretch. He was absolutely shattered, and yet he was still in the mood for jokes. He claimed that he had been seduced on the way be a *yeti* woman—and kept a very straight face in telling us this! But he did admit that at times he had really thought he wouldn't make it.

One thing was clear. A three-man rope, including Eric, would be too much of a burden on our ascent. We couldn't possibly allow ourselves so much time without running the risk of getting into serious danger. Eric rec-

Unknown mountains over 19,700 feet high, southeast of Pangboche.

ognized this and therefore declined to use the two oxygen cylinders that had been deposited for us at the South Col. He felt it would not have been sporting and said he preferred to stay in the camp and film our departure and our return.

The night became icy cold. In spite of three layers of sleeping bags, our hands and feet froze pitifully. We crawled together as closely as possible. Again I asked myself how on earth Reinhold had managed to survive the two nights up here, exposed to the storm, without any damage to his health. It was impossible to sleep, and at three o'clock in the morning, Reinhold set about brewing some tea again. We wanted to take in another three or four quarts of fluid, but it took ages before he had managed to convert the necessary amount of snow into water for the tea.

Eric reacted to my attempts to wake him with fearful grunting noises. You really might have believed that he was taking his pleasure with a *yeti* woman in his dreams!

In the meantime it had reached half past five. We got ourselves ready in the tent and attached our crampons; then we went outside. It was the eighth of May 1978. Today we would either conquer the summit or abandon the whole idea forever, because we wanted above all to avoid spending another night between the South Col and the main summit as the others had done. Therefore, we would have to conquer the remaining 2,782 feet in one single mighty effort. At least we have one advantage, I thought, we don't need to worry whether or not our oxygen is going to last. Yet, at the same time, I had to wonder at my own stupidity. Already I was suffering badly from the altitude. I was lethargic, my feet were like lead and I had absolutely no drive at all. If my condition worsened, I wouldn't even manage to get to the South Summit.

But the doubts of the past days had completely disappeared. I no longer thought of home, of my wife and child, but only of one thing—the mountaineering difficulties that lay ahead. I was concentrating solely on the ascent, registering each of my steps, and trying to pace myself as much as possible. One can hardly boast of any exalted thoughts or feelings. My whole field of vision was very narrow, and confined itself to the absolutely necessary. I saw only my feet, the next steps and handholds. I was moving automatically. I "switched off" completely, and thought only of the next five feet in front of me. I didn't think of Everest. I didn't think of our goal. Only that I had to put those five feet behind me—that alone was important, and nothing else. If I thought of anything else at all, then it was how I was best going to get down from here.

The air became thinner and thinner, and I was near to suffocation. I still remember the words that went through my mind, matching the rhythm of my steps: "Go on, go on, go on." It was like a Tibetan prayer wheel. Mechanically I put one foot down in front of the other.

12

I N THE FIRST phase of the ascent Reinhold had gained a small lead. While I was still trying to wake Eric Jones, he had already gone on. We wanted to go up to the South Summit without a rope. Reinhold was carrying a fifty-foot rope on his rucksack, which we would use at the very top. I had my camera equipment with me, reserve clothing, goggles, as well as a small amount of food.

Shortly before beginning the steep ascent that leads up to the southeast ridge, I saw Reinhold. He was sitting on a rock plateau and was looking toward me. From this point on we made a track together and took the lead alternately. The flank on which we found ourselves was filled with such large snowdrifts that we sank into them up to our hips. Then extremely thick fog came up and we were afraid that we would lose sight of each other. We were now at exactly the same height as Mallory and Irvine had been before they disappeared forever from the view of their comrades in the fog. This thought shot through my mind as we rested. On looking back, I have the impression that I spoke to Reinhold about this, but that isn't true. We never exchanged a single word, mainly because we were far too short of breath. Nevertheless, the memory of a conversation between us is very vivid indeed. I believe that we were as close to each other spiritually then as two people possibly can be. Perhaps this was because of the fact that during these hours we must have been the loneliest people in the whole world.

Much has been written about the fact that at extreme altitudes, like those of Everest, the veil that hides the great beyond is particularly thin, so thin that even completely normal people have supernatural experiences of which they otherwise only read in ghost stories. There is a saying that whoever is killed up on the mountain wanders forever after his death, and guides the living mountaineers during their last feet to the summit.

One English mountaineer suddenly found himself in the company of six Asiatics. This was shortly after the six Russian mountaineers were lost while ascending to the summit. There had been, in fact, Asiatics among them, but at that time nobody had heard about the disappearance of the six men.

Another climber once suddenly found himself face to face with an Englishman in old-fashioned climbing togs, who had suddenly appeared out of the fog and walked toward him. The two men shared a piece of cake with each other before the unknown apparition disappeared again without trace.

The most haunting description of such an apparition comes from the pen of Nick Estcourt. He was a member

Pages 168–169
Mount Everest seen from the west. Left, the northeast ridge; in the foreground, the southeast ridge.

of Chris Bonington's last expedition to Everest, during which, in spite of oxygen and modern equipment, Mick Burke disappeared on the summit, never to be seen again.

Nick Estcourt's experience is set down in Chris Bonington's book *Everest the Hard Way:*

I went on alone toward half past three in the morning, and pulled myself up on the fixed ropes which led to Camp V. It was a clear, moonlit night and the contours of the rocks stood out clearly against the white snow. I was about 200 feet above Camp IV when I turned round. I don't know why I did that— perhaps it was because I sensed somebody was following me. In any case I turned round, and it was then that I discovered this figure behind me. He looked like a normal mountaineer, and he was far enough behind me so that I couldn't feel his movements on the fixed rope. I made out arms and legs and assumed that it was somebody who wanted to catch me up. I stopped and waited. Thereupon he, too, seemed to stop and didn't wave or give any sort of sign, so I thought that I might just as well go on. I now wondered whether it could perhaps be Ang Phurbe, ascending from Camp II, to surprise us all when we reached Camp V in the morning. I climbed on, turning round three or four times, and each time this figure was still there behind me. . . . It was quite unmistakably a human being with arms and legs, and I remember his body once disappeared up to his hips in a gentle trough. When I reached the site of the former Camp IV, I turned round again but nobody was there any more. It seemed uncanny. He couldn't possibly in that short time have turned round and slid down the rope, especially since I could clearly look back at the route down into the new Camp IV. The whole episode was very strange.

In 1933, Frank Smythe had reported that he was convinced that during his attempted solo assault on Everest he was linked by his rope with a second man. Smythe found himself at that time without oxygen at an altitude of around 26,000 feet. Possibly he was having hallucinations. But Nick Estcourt was still below the 26,000-foot barrier and, what is more, with oxygen. He was well adapted to the altitude, a sober man with the analytical intelligence of a mathematician. A hallucination seems in his case to be completely out of the question. He had seen the apparition precisely at that place where in 1973, his friend, Jangbo, had been killed in an avalanche, and a few hours before the disappearance of Mick Burke.

In all seriousness, Bonington was of the opinion that Nick Estcourt had had a parapsychic experience, which was in some way connected with a tragic accident in the past or the future.

Herbert Tichy, who himself had a similar experience, writes: "Things like this arise because the spirit has somehow broken free from the anchorage which holds it fast far down in the valley, and strays right up to the very frontiers of insanity."

A more sober, but nonetheless fantastic, interpretation of these phenomena, would connect them with the story of the *yeti*, the so-called Abominable Snowman. A few scientists are of the opinion that he really exists. Eric Shipton even photographed his tracks at an altitude of 19,000 feet, and later published the photographs. According to one theory, the *yeti* is a descendant of the gigantopithecus, an enormous ape-man whose fossilized jaw-

Pages 172–173
View of the Kang Taiga (22,200 feet), left, and the Tamserku (21,700 feet), right, in the Khumbu Himal.

The Kang Taiga (22,200 feet) in the Khumbu Himal.

bones have been found in South China and India. He lived there half a million years ago before fleeing from the first humans into the mountains, where he still lives on quietly today. There are innumerable stories about the *yeti,* and in many monasteries you can find pictorial representations of him.

I don't believe in ghosts or fables, and I am fully convinced that most of these stories can be explained by the presence of an overwrought imagination. In this lonely environment, which is so hostile to life, the imagination conjures up all manner of strange desires or horrifying apparitions.

But not everything can simply be rationally explained away. For example, not the feeling that you are talking to a human being who, in reality, is not saying a word, but who is nevertheless, simultaneously reacting to unspoken thoughts. I mention this now because I can remember most clearly our own situation at that time. Nothing would have surprised me then. Everything seemed to be totally normal; I had completely lost the feeling of being in the Himalayas and of climbing Everest. I could just as well have been on the Mosele or the Ahornspitze at home. The fog cloaked everything, and made us forget both the vastness and the greatness of our surroundings. We were traversing a steep snowfield, which had to be tracked step by step. Occasionally I stopped, rammed the ice ax into the snow and leaned on it for a quarter or half a minute, gasping for breath and trying to recover. Then, somehow, I would gain a new strength and could go on for ten or twenty more steps. Strangely, after I had put behind me a few hundred feet of altitude, I no longer felt so lethargic. On the contrary, everything seemed to go more easily. Perhaps this was owing to the fact that we were getting better accustomed to this unimaginable altitude.

Naturally, wading through deep snow did represent an enormous drain on our strength. Where possible, we made a detour onto ice-covered rock where the wind had blown away the layer of snow. Although, technically, it is much more difficult to climb over rock that is iced up than it is to find a track through deep snow, it seemed to us to be easier. We had to concentrate so hard on every foothold and every handhold that there was no time left to think about our exhaustion.

After four hours, toward half past nine, we stood in front of the tents of Camp V at an altitude of 27,900 feet. Mallory and Irvine, too, had managed to get this far. From now on we would be entering completely new territory. We were left totally to our own resources. If anything happened to us now, no rescue team would be able to come up to help us, no helicopter—nothing. The smallest accident would mean certain death.

Reinhold and I had often spoken together about the fact that, in this last phase, it would be impossible to help each other should anything untoward occur. Although we were incredibly close to each other, and formed an indivisible unit, we were agreed on one thing. If one of us should get into difficulty, the other would have to try at all costs to find safety for himself alone. The small amount of strength that remained to each of us was hardly enough for one; any attempt to rescue or even to recover another person would be doomed to failure.

I sat in front of the small tent, half covered by snow, while inside Reinhold tried desperately to get a stove going to brew up tea. I snuggled up to the side of the tent in order to rest a bit in the lee side, and stared out into the fog. Occasionally the wall of fog would lift for a moment, and I could see far below me the Valley of Silence. I could see the Lhotse, and again and again I looked up to the South Summit where an enormous trail of snow signified that up there a far more violent storm was raging than down here in Camp V. The weather would undoubtedly worsen. The fine weather period was over.

Perhaps our attempt on the summit was finally over, too, our Everest expedition wrecked once and for all. Of one thing I was convinced: I would never come up here a second time. Already the desire to turn back was almost overpowering. To bivouac here in Camp V, and perhaps to wait for the weather to improve, was also completely out of the question. We would probably never have got out of the tent at all again, and in no event would we have had the physical or mental strength to climb any farther. Our energy would have lasted at the most for the descent and no more. Yet climbing on was, under these circumstances, also a "way of no return."

In 1956, two Japanese had mastered the route from the South Col to the summit in one go. This had taken them a whole day, and having therefore reached the main summit late in the afternoon, they were forced to bivouac on the way back. Consequently, in spite of carrying oxygen, they had suffered terrible injuries through frostbite. But neither Reinhold nor I had time to think of these dangers. The will to push on blotted out everything else, even the wish to turn back or at least to sleep. We wanted in any case to go on up, even if we could only reach the South Summit, which is 28,608 feet high. After all, even to conquer the South Summit without oxygen, would have been a tremendous success. It would have proved that one day it would be possible to reach the main summit by human strength alone.

It took exactly half an hour for Reinhold to prepare the tea. My deliberations were also shared by him; we exchanged them wordlessly. We were completely united in our determination to continue the assault on the summit.

Once again we set off. The tracks of our predecessors, which could still be seen in the snow, served as an excellent orientation guide. The clouds were moving over from the southwest, from the bad weather corner of the Himalayas. We had to push ourselves even more because that promised bad news. We found ourselves in the lower reaches of the jet stream, those raging winds of speeds up to 124 miles per hour upon which the enormous passenger planes are carried from continent to continent. We had traversed the troposphere and were approaching the frontier of the stratosphere. Here cosmic radiation is multiplied. Only a few minutes without our snow goggles sufficed even in the fog to diminish our powers of vision. In a very short space of time direct insolation would lead to snow blindness and painful conjunctivitis.

Reinhold and I photographed and filmed as often as we had the opportunity. To do this, we had to take off our snow goggles and we also had to remove our overgloves. Each time it became more difficult for us to put the gloves back on again. But losing them would have led to the very rapid paralysis and frostbite of our hands.

Since it was no longer possible to go on in this deep snow, we had made a detour toward the southeast ridge. Here the wall dropped 6,500 feet down to the southwest. One false step and we would have plunged down into the Valley of Silence. The exposed, very airy climb on brittle rock without any rope demanded extreme concentration. Reinhold was right behind me. I took the lead to the South Summit. Completely without warning, we suddenly found we had passed through the clouds and now stood on the summit approach of the mountain, the last stage before our goal.

At this point the storm attacked us with all its might and forced us back. However, in spite of the storm and the fatigue my fear of the mountain had dissipated with the clouds. I was quite sure of myself. Over there lay the main summit, almost near enough to touch, and at this precise moment I was sure we were going to do it, Reinhold, too, told me later: "This was the moment in which I was convinced of the definitive success of our adventure."

A sort of joyful intoxication overcame the two of us. We looked at each other—and shrank back. From Reinhold's appearance I could only conclude that my own was very similar. His face was contorted in a grimace, his mouth wide open while he gasped, panting for air. Icicles hung in his beard. His face was almost without human traits. Our physical reserves were exhausted. We were so

Pages 180–181
Left, Mount Everest; right, the Nuptse (26,000 feet).

utterly spent that we scarcely had the strength to take ten paces in one go. Again and again we had to stop, but nothing in the world could have held us back now.

We had roped ourselves together because the summit ridge, as Hillary has already described it, was overhung by great cornices. It is true, however, that in an emergency a rope would not have helped us.

We crawled forward at a snail's pace, trusting to instinct alone. The sun glistened on the snow and the sky above the summit was of such an intense blue that it seemed almost black. We were very close to the sky and it was only with our own strength alone that we had arrived up here at the seat of the gods.

13

REINHOLD SIGNALED to me with a movement of his hand that he wanted to go on ahead. He wanted to film me climbing up over the ridge, with the bubbling sea of clouds below.

To do this he had to take off his snow goggles in order to focus the camera better. It occurred to me that his eyes looked inflamed, but I thought nothing more of it, no more than he did. Our altitude was now 28,500 feet, and we had obviously reached a point at which normal brain functions had broken down, or at least were severely limited. Our attentiveness and concentration declined; our instinct no longer reacted as reliably as before; the capacity for clear logical thinking had also apparently been lost. I only thought in sensations and loose associations, and slowly I was overcome by the feeling that this threatening fearful mountain could, in fact, be a friend, if only I could understand him properly.

Today I am certain that it is in these positive and friendly sensations that the real danger on Everest lies. When one approaches the summit, one no longer perceives the hostile, the absolutely deadly atmosphere that has penetrated before. I have probably never been so close to death as I was during this last hour before reaching the summit, not even that time on the Wilder Kaiser mountain when I fell 100 feet down the rope in a free-fall, and miraculously survived unhurt. Then at least I was still aware of the danger of death, but now I was not. The urgent compulsion to descend again, to give in to fatigue, that had overcome me already in Camp V, and which body and soul had rebelled against, the feeling of this being a deadly and threatening adventure, had disappeared. I was now feeling the complete opposite. I had been seized by a real sense of euphoria. I felt somehow light and relaxed, and believed that nothing could happen to me. Undoubtedly many of the men who have disappeared forever in the summit region of Everest had also fallen victim to this treacherous euphoria. I can well imagine Mick Burke sitting happily smiling on the summit, and thinking to himself, "How beautiful it all is up here; I'd like to stay here." And then his life was snuffed out like the flame of a candle. It must have been exactly the same with him. At this altitude the boundaries between life and death are fluid. I wandered along this narrow ridge, and perhaps for a few seconds I had indeed gone beyond the frontier that divides life from death. By a piece of good fortune I was allowed to return. I would not risk it a second time, my reason forbids me to gamble with my life in such a way again.

After our return, Reinhold and I were hailed as victors over Everest, but this is false. Everest was neither conquered nor overcome by us—it simply tolerated us. And if we can talk about a victory at all, then it is at the most a victory over our own bodies, over fear.

It was a very personal, lonely victory in a struggle that each of us fought alone, and the victory was not achieved in the last feet that still lay before us. It had already been achieved at the moment when we took the first step out into the unknown. And it was secured and documented when we returned alive from the kingdom of the dead.

In spite of all my euphoria, I was physically completely finished. I was no longer walking of my own free will, but mechanically, like an automaton. I seemed to step outside myself, and had the illusion that another person was walking in my place. This other person arrived at the Hillary Step, that perilous eighty-two-foot high ridge gradient, and then climbed and pulled himself up in the footsteps of his predecessors. He had one foot in Tibet and the other in Nepal. On the left side there was a 6500-foot descent to Nepal; on the right the wall dropped 13,000 feet down toward China. We were alone, this one other person and myself. Although he was connected to me by the short length of rope, Reinhold no longer existed.

This feeling of being outside myself was interrupted for only a few moments. A cramp in my right hand bent my fingers together, and tore me violently back to reality. I was attacked by a suffocating fear of death. "Now I've had it." This thought went through my head, "Now the lack of oxygen is beginning its deadly work."

I could see the Sherpa in front of me who, a few days ago, had been brought down to the base camp. With him, too, it had started this way, and by the time the doctors had attended to him, he was already paralyzed on one side. Presumably he would never recover again properly. Nevertheless—he was alive; he was rescued. But up here that was impossible. I massaged my right forearm, I bent my fingers back, turned my hand and then the cramp eased.

From then on I prayed, "Lord God, let me go up right to the top. Give me the power to remain alive, don't let me die up here." I crawled on my elbows and knees and prayed uninterruptedly, more fervently than I ever had done in my life before. It was like a dialogue with a higher being. And again I saw myself crawling up, below me, beside me, higher and higher. I was being pushed up high, and then suddenly I was up again on my own two feet: I was standing on the summit.

It was one fifteen in the afternoon of the eighth of May 1978.

And then suddenly Reinhold was with me too, still carrying his camera, at the three-legged Chinese surveying instrument. We had arrived. We embraced each other. We sobbed and stammered, and could not keep calm. The tears poured from under my goggles into my beard, froze on my cheeks. We embraced each other again and again. We pressed each other close. We stepped back at arm's length and again fell round each others' necks, laughing and crying at the same time. We were redeemed and liberated, freed at last from the inhuman compulsion to climb on.

After the crying and the sense of redemption, came the emptiness and the sadness, the disappointment. Something had been taken from me; something that had been very important to me. Something that had suffused my whole being had evaporated, and I now felt exhausted and hollow. There was no feeling of triumph or victory. I saw the surrounding summits, the Lhotse, the Cho Oyu. The view toward Tibet was obscured by clouds. I knew that I was standing now on the highest point in the whole world. But, somehow, it was all a matter of indifference to me. I just wanted to get home now, back to that world from which I had come, and as fast as possible.

I cut off a piece of the rope that still connected me to Reinhold, and tied the three-foot-long end to the Chinese surveying tripod as proof that we had been up here. The Bull and Reinhard Karl later brought the piece of rope down with them again.

After taking a couple of photos of Reinhold, I was driven on by an irresistible urge to descend. I said to Reinhold, "I'm going." We had established during our ascent that, in fact, we didn't need the rope. We could, therefore, easily descend separately. He wanted to stay up a while longer and take a few pictures. He had also intended to speak a few words into a tape recorder, simply to establish whether, at an altitude of 29,028 feet, you are still able to formulate and conceive clear thoughts. I had no idea how much the cosmic radiation had affected him, and he, too, knew very little about it, otherwise we would scarcely have separated, but would have descended together. Only one thing was important to me now, to get back to Camp IV as safely and as quickly as possible.

Reinhold had asked me to leave the rope at the Hillary Step, but this projects up into a snowy ridge. It would have been impossible for me to anchor the rope securely without leaving behind my ice ax. I decided to go down without a rope, knowing then that Reinhold would be able to manage it as well. So I took the rope with me.

There was nothing heroic about the descent, any more than there had been about the ascent. I had been guided up by a power that I cannot define, and now I ran down, driven on by the pure naked will to survive. The quicker I descended, the greater were my chances of surviving this adventure without damaging my health. I did not know how much my organs and my brain had already been affected. I didn't know whether I was the same man who had climbed up here in the first place, but I sensed that I had regained my freedom of action, which had escaped me for a short time during the ascent.

In a flash I had the Hillary Step behind me. I had traversed the summit ridge, and now attempted to climb up the counter-gradient to the South Summit. And then something happened that I had already experienced in earlier expeditions. During a descent it is almost impossible to cope with even the smallest counter-gradient. "Power is gone," I thought as I allowed myself to sink down into the snow before the South Summit. I literally crawled up on all fours, reached the summit, turned round and saw Reinhold, who had just put the Hillary Step behind him. In the process I must have even taken some photos, because when I got home again and developed my films, this scene had been captured: Reinhold below the Hillary Step. But I don't remember at all how I raised the camera, adjusted the distance or pressed the trigger. Yet if this gap in my memory is the only lasting damage I have suffered, then I have every reason to be thankful.

On the South Summit I decided not to descend by the normal route, via the southeast ridge, but to glissade down the east flank. I, therefore, sat down in the snow, and then simply slid down the precipice, using the ice ax as a sort of rudder and braking with my feet. But before setting off, I marked out in the snow with the handle of my ice ax three or four arrows in a downward direction to show Reinhold the way in which I had descended. He apparently did see these arrows, but didn't want to take any risks, and so chose the more difficult route via the ridge. I, on the other hand, didn't think of the danger of avalanches; nor did I consider the fact that beneath me the wall dropped steeply for 13,000 feet. Only one thing was important to me, and that was to get the dangerous death zone behind me as quickly as possible. I was anxious to arrive at the safety of the tents of Camp IV, where Eric Jones was probably still waiting for us.

I managed the 650 feet to the altitude of Camp V in one slide on the seat of my pants. Beneath me a comfortable pillow of snow had formed, on which I slid down to the valley as on a cushion. Then I stood up, traversed the southeast ridge, and repeated the whole maneuver again at Camp V. This time, however, I had to be more cautious, because I had to stop occasionally and descend over the rock walls that we had clambered up during the ascent. Curiously enough, I didn't seem to gain any relief from the air that was gradually becoming denser; on the contrary, I somehow felt that the air was becoming, if anything, even thinner than during the ascent. My legs trembled on the rock traverses and my heart beat wildly.

Shortly above the South Col, that is to say shortly before my goal, I sprang from a rock into the snow. In doing this a shelf of snow gave way. Now things went more quickly than I really wanted. I turned a couple of somersaults, losing my ice ax and protective goggles. My crampons were also torn from my boots. I found the irons later; they were still hanging firmly from the straps. Then suddenly I became aware of a searing pain in my right ankle. I must have struck it against a stone.

But, in spite of this turbulent descent, I arrived below safe and sound. Eric Jones was already there. He had observed my crazy descent and feared the worst. He had thought that the whole thing was developing into a real avalanche from which I would be unable to escape. He had left the camp and had come toward me to help. To his great amazement, I stood up and hobbled painfully toward him. I embraced Eric and stammered, "We climbed Everest without oxygen." Again I was moved to tears, this time from exhaustion.

But Eric couldn't share my emotion. He just looked at me with an indescribable expression on his face, almost as if he had seen a ghost. Only after a while did I understand why. I must have looked dreadful. I had split open my forehead and it was bleeding. I had lost my goggles and my eyes were coated with ice. My nose was deep blue, almost black from cold, and my beard was snow-white. Emaciated and hollow-cheeked, I must have looked like a living corpse. Reinhold looked exactly the same when he staggered into the camp an hour later.

I rushed into the tent, grabbed hold of the radio set and shouted into it, "We reached the summit without oxygen!" It was all the same to me whether anybody heard me or not. But I simply had to shout it out to the whole world. However, Bull was in Camp II at the set, which had been tuned in to reception the whole time in the event of our return. He answered me with a wild shriek. Through the radio I heard a colossal din in the camp. We were told later that the whole team had got absolutely sozzled with Kukri rum at the news of our success. They never stopped toasting us and singing our praises. But really this rejoicing was premature, since we were not yet out of the danger zone. Something still faced us which I will never forget for the rest of my life.

I had stood at the summit with Reinhold at 1:15 P.M., and a quarter of an hour later I had set off on the return journey. I now discovered from Eric that the time was 2:30 P.M., and I had therefore managed the trek from the summit to Camp IV in just one hour, whereas for the ascent we had taken almost eight hours.

Reinhold arrived half an hour later. I don't know how he found the camp. It was a real miracle because he was suffering from snow blindness. His eyes were red and inflamed, and he couldn't even see the teacup that I held toward him. I have once had an attack of snow blindness myself, but this exceeded anything that I had ever seen. We really feared the worst, because Bull had established during routine examinations that, after stays at a great altitude, mild hemorrhages would appear in the retina of the eye. Was Reinhold's blindness, perhaps, not only due to the snow, but also the result of a massive hemorrhage? Or did it show up an incipient cerebral edema? This was a really serious worry. On top of this, Reinhold was suffering agonizing pain in his eyes, which drove him half mad. We didn't even have eye ointment or pain-killing drugs with us. Either no medicaments had been brought up, or they had been used up and not replenished. I only had my usual, very powerful pain-killing tablets with me, which I always carry around. I gave three of them to Reinhold, whose condition was getting worse and worse.

14

THROUGHOUT the night Reinhold screamed with pain, sobbing and crying. He implored me again and again, "Don't leave me alone, Peter. Please, you must stay with me. Don't go; don't climb down alone without me!" You see, he was naturally thinking of our agreement that if one of us became ill, then the healthy partner must try to save himself. But for me there was no question of this: "I won't leave you alone, Reinhold. Please believe me. I'll stay with you and we'll go down together. We'll manage that, don't worry. Eric will help us."

I kept from him the fact that Eric was also not in very good shape. He had frostbite of his fingers and toes, and had become very apathetic and lethargic due to the altitude. He would certainly not be much help. Perhaps he even needed help himself.

I alone had complete responsibility for my two friends, just as Reinhold alone had had responsibility for the two Sherpas. And, as had happened then, suddenly a mighty storm blew up. It whistled and howled over the South Col, shaking the tents wildly. On top of this I had to listen to the sobbing and entreaties of Reinhold, and again I prayed, this time for my friend.

Reinhold knows that occasionally I say a prayer. I am a believer, even if I am not particularly pious. And to be honest, I must admit that I only pray in emergency situations. I believe that I draw strength from prayer. Reinhold has always found this rather amusing. It's not that he has laughed at me; that he would never do. At the most he simply smiles gently, because Reinhold doesn't believe in any God. He finds praying superfluous, he believes that he draws strength only from himself, and that no outside power contributes anything to it.

He is not yet even ready to discuss the question of whether perhaps additional powers can be mobilized that are normally blocked. I once told him about a fall in the Alps, during which I plunged down over a steep snowfield covered with large stones, having been dragged down by another mountaineer. While I was falling, I prayed that I wouldn't be smashed to pieces on a boulder, and when I reached the bottom I got up unhurt. Well, Reinhold believes that that would have happened to me anyway, even if I hadn't prayed.

I must, it's true, admit that basically I only know Reinhold as a mountaineer; as a human being he has always remained an enigma to me. I have often told him about myself and my motives, about my doubts and fears, my hopes and my longings. And, although he has always listened attentively, he has revealed almost nothing at all about himself. Only once did he open up somewhat, when he confessed to me that he looked for adventure at high altitudes and in distant lands in order to find himself: "I have to come here where other yardsticks apply, where a man is still a man, where one is reduced to what is fundamental and quite elementary. Only then am I at one with myself."

Insofar as this is true, Reinhold is basically an untroubled and free human being who risks all in order to win all. He is a man who builds only on himself, on his own strength and on his own ability. It is in this that we differ. Thus, I believe that a heartfelt prayer does have its profound meaning. I can imagine that in praying, one somehow invokes all the good forces that are in us and around us.

I had no illusions about our present situation. The conquest of the summit had used up a great deal of our physical strength. The storm might detain us up here for a long time, and nobody would be able, in this sort of weather, to come up to us from below. We were completely left to our own resources. It was worse, much worse, than that time in Camp II when I had been the prey of so much fear. Now I had no fear. Perhaps my senses were too dulled. Perhaps also I'd somehow got used to living with danger. I don't know. In any case, this night of storms and pain in Camp IV somehow tore more at my nerves than at my heart.

Reinhold was sitting upright because the pains were more bearable in this position than when he was lying down. I kept brewing tea for him, and tried to ease his discomfort as far as I could. I myself felt quite well and capable of putting up with all sorts of physical hardships. And at no time did the thought occur to me that I could abandon Reinhold and descend without him. During the night I felt more bound to him than ever before.

Finally dawn broke. I couldn't feel my feet anymore,

and I feared that frostbite had set in. Reinhold still had the same bad pains as during the night. He was still unable to see, which frightened him a great deal. In spite of my assurances to the contrary, he was afraid that I would abandon him to his fate, alone up here. I knew we had to get down immediately. We had to, because we could not have survived another day and night.

I helped Reinhold to dress, and, at six o'clock in the morning of May 9, we left the tent. Now for the first time I noticed that my eyesight was hazy. During my turbulent slide down through the snow, I had lost my goggles and had been exposed for some time to the very strong ultraviolet rays. I hoped desperately that I wouldn't suffer so much as Reinhold. Besides, my ankle was causing me hellish pain, so we just had to get down fast.

Reinhold and I left the tent first, and Eric followed. Step by step, we groped our way via the South Col over to the Lhotse Face. The storm hit us with its full force, and the weather seemed even colder. But now I wasn't only responsible for myself, and this helped me forget my own unhappiness.

We reached the fixed ropes that were hanging on the Lhotse Face. We then clipped the belaying snap-links onto the ropes, which were anchored in the rock and ice. First of all we had to overcome two long traverses on the wall before we could descend vertically. In spite of his miserable condition, Reinhold managed to descend to Camp II under his own steam. Although scarcely in command of his senses anymore, he somehow conquered the wall with the sureness of a sleepwalker. I could not help him make the descent, nor could Eric, who had his own problems to overcome. At this point, Reinhold really benefited from his many years of training, which had turned all his movements on the mountain into mere reflexes.

Another thing that stood him in good stead was his fantastic mountaineering talent. I can still remember the first time I met Reinhold. He was eighteen and I was twenty. At that time he was sporting an American crew cut and was simply a boy who, like myself, had climbed all over the mountains of our homeland. I met him in the South Tyrol during a climbing tour with Sepp Mayerl, and at first sight one couldn't really see anything special in him. Yet, although he was the youngest in our group, somehow I recognized even then his uncompromising toughness and his daring.

Whenever others wanted to give up because of some worsening of the weather, he would say, "We'll try it nevertheless." And if nobody wanted to go with him, then he went solo.

This remark of his, "we'll try it nevertheless," became typical of Reinhold in the years ahead. Even at first I noticed that I had a sort of temperamental affinity to him. Just like me, he refused to climb up mountains as if he were a sort of locksmith. He didn't want to just bang one ice piton after another into the rock face, and hammer and nail his way up the mountain as was then the practice. He wanted to climb—to climb freely—even in difficult terrain, and, if possible, without a rope.

We didn't know, of course, at that time that we would one day undertake together a series of the most difficult expeditions, but we got on well with each other. We teamed up again and again on combined tours and gradually discovered that we formed an ideal team. By different routes we had reached the same conclusion. We had established how important it is not only to be safe on a mountain, but also to be fast. We set our goals higher and higher until, with Everest, we finally conquered our highest goal of all.

We reached Camp III in the early hours of the morning. It was empty. We simply crawled into the tent and hoped that soon the sun would break through and warm us. In the first-aid kit I found eyedrops and an ointment against snow blindness. I attended to Reinhold as best I could as he was still suffering from terrible pains. Finally, we even slept a little.

The sun woke us up at nine o'clock. Shortly after this we heard voices. It was the Bull and Reinhard Karl. We were particularly delighted that Bull of all people should be the first member of the expedition to come toward us. Bull had always followed our venture with special sympathy. He had encouraged us, and also reassured us with regard to the medical problems. He had become a true friend.

Bull examined us. Apparently he was quite satisfied with the results of his examination. He gave Reinhold some eyedrops and also some pain-killing tablets. At the same time he supplied me with tips and advice as to how I could continue to help Reinhold, and best get him back to the base camp. I was very moved, too, by the attention Reinhard Karl showed us. Although he was shattered and exhausted by the ascent, he brewed tea for us and supported us wherever possible.

Dr. Ölz on the last few feet to the summit.

Reinhold and I remained in Camp III for about three hours, and then we continued our descent. Bull and Reinhard Karl spent the night here in order to begin their attack on the summit the next morning. We wished them much luck.

We couldn't know then that the ascent of Everest by Dr. Ölz and Reinhard Karl would be very important for us. We told both of them that the two oxygen cylinders that we had taken with us for safety's sake (in case of an emergency involving members of our party) were lying in Camp IV untouched. We thought that they would be very useful to them during their ascent. As Bull and Reinhard later repeatedly confirmed, they found our two cylinders in Camp IV, completely full. This was the most convincing proof that we had really ascended the summit of Everest without oxygen, and was to be crucial to us in defending ourselves against the reproaches and accusations that were later leveled at us. Bull also brought with him the piece of rope that I had left behind at the summit.

The assertion that we had cheated during our ascent without oxygen is untenable for other reasons as well. Our expedition consisted of eleven men, and in such cases it is completely impossible to conceal any dishonesty within the team. The oxygen cylinders that we carried with us were counted and strictly divided up. It would have been impossible for anyone to have secretly got hold of a cylinder. It often happens that individual members of an expedition, or even Sherpas, use up more oxygen than foreseen. This in fact amounts to a small-scale catastrophe, because if, in high altitudes, even one single cylinder is missing, this can jeopardize the success of an entire summit assault.

Finally, some experts reproached us with the fact that, although we had not used oxygen during the entire ascent, we had, on the other hand, allowed ourselves a sniff of it at least at intervals. Above all, according to them, we had used our breathing equipment at night. But, medically speaking, this would have been an impossibility. Either you go with oxygen or without it. Once your body has accustomed itself to the lack of oxygen, a sudden flood of oxygen would prove disastrous, and would, in fact, lead to an immediate collapse.

The accusations that were made against Reinhold and myself after our return to Europe are, therefore, completely fabricated. They show, however, that an achievement like ours immediately provokes envy and jealousy, whether it be for the sake of sporting competition or downright financial interests.

The rest pause in Camp III had in fact brought us very little relief. I was still utterly exhausted and my legs were still trembling, but we were going down. The prospect of reaching the advanced base camp in the foreseeable future kept us going.

Late in the afternoon we were again on the Lhotse Face. The fixed ropes guided us to the foot of the wall. Then we had to overcome a flat but very difficult stretch. We no longer roped ourselves together. However, I gave Reinhold the end of my ski pole so that he could steady himself with it. In this way, I led him carefully over the ice, past the countless glacier crevasses. Still he could see hardly anything. And again and again he had to take a pause to rest.

"I can't go on, I'll never get any farther," he said. He saw ice crevasses where there were none. He was completely confused and was suffering from hallucinations. But we simply could not stop. We were not yet by any means out of the death zone.

If night should surprise us on the way, we would be lost. Neither Reinhold nor I could have survived a bivouac out in the open. We were far too weak for that. We simply had to keep going. And, as Reinhold had once driven on the Sherpas, so now I drove him on. I allowed him no rest. I forced him to his feet and forward whenever he wanted to give up. While doing this, of course, I would much rather have sat down next to him myself. I had somehow to feign strength and determination, although I, too, was at the end of my tether. My whole body was hurting me, my injured ankle was causing me hellish pain at every step and my brain was dulled. If I felt so wretched, how much worse was Reinhold's position—completely helpless and reliant on my guidance!

Thus we stumbled on for two-and-a-half hours, until finally, like a fata morgana, the colorful tents of the advanced base camp loomed up before us. Jubilant, concerned, helping Sherpas rushed toward us. There was tea, a lot of tea, and still more tea. We were so dried out, so dehydrated that our faces looked like those of old men.

I couldn't imagine that on the next day we would be able to descend to the base camp. I calculated that we would need at least two to three days to recover sufficiently before being able to traverse, for the eighteenth and last time, the treacherous Khumbu Icefall without endangering our lives.

During the night I tended to Reinhold again with more ointment and drops. We drank still more tea. We also slept a little at intervals, and in the morning we realized that we could do it; we could reach the base camp.

The route from Camp II to Camp I through the Valley of Silence confronted us once again with a difficult test. But we pushed on at a good pace, in spite of my ankle, which caused me so much pain now that I seriously believed that I must have broken something. Reinhold was feeling much better. He was able, at least, to see contours and his optimism had returned. Without looking either to right or left, we climbed finally through the icefall.

Ladders, ropes and more ladders, and then around

midday we were in the base camp, and hobbled through the victory arch, which our comrades had set up for us. For the first time I was overcome by a feeling of genuine pride.

Journalists were there. They had flown over from Europe, specially to experience the great event at first hand. The two people from *Stern* magazine, who had been flown in by helicopter, looked rather pale. The altitude was causing them a lot of problems. Once again, it proved how foolhardy it is to expose oneself to such a change without acclimatization. Journalists from England and also Austria had arrived. We were surrounded and besieged; question after question showered down upon us. Meanwhile the Kukri rum, which had been kept for our return, was making the rounds, and somebody said, in between two mighty slugs: "You'll see, nobody will believe you, nobody." Reinhold threw back his head and laughed. He was almost the old Reinhold again. Interviews and strobe lights, as well as mountains, put him in his element. He related to the smallest detail how the ascent and descent had gone, while I retired into my tent. The photographs on the tent poles made me think of my home again for the first time.

A little later I wrote a long letter to my friend, Ernst Spiess:

Base Camp
May 11, 1978

My Dear Ernst,

I still can't grasp that our goal—to conquer Everest without oxygen—has been reached. It seems to me that we were on any old mountain and not on the highest one in the whole world. Insofar as one can now assess it, neither Reinhold nor I has suffered any serious physical or, what is more important, mental damage. We did get a bit of frostbite on our fingers and toes—after all there were temperatures of minus 35 degrees [minus 31 degrees Fahrenheit], plus winds of roughly 80 kilometers [50 miles per hour] on the summit ridge. But Manni says it will be okay. There are a few lapses in memory, but we have no other mental deficiencies, and nothing is likely to come later. (At least that's what doctors Ölz and Manni say.)

I don't know where I should start my story. You will probably have read something in the *Kronenzeitung,* but don't believe a word of it. I'll try to give you in short form a description of the basic events.

. . . On the eighth of May Reinhold began cooking at three o'clock in the morning, and we drank about two liters of liquid. It is most important to keep the blood flowing. It was 38 degrees [36 degrees Fahrenheit] below zero. At about half past four we got ourselves ready to set off. We had only about three or four kilos of gear in our rucksacks (reserve gloves, goggles, etc). At 5.15 we crawled out of the tent, and saw that the weather looked bad in the west. A solid bank of cloud had formed. We decided, however, to set off despite this. . . . Both of us noticed the lack of oxygen immediately, the more so because there was a lot of drifting snow through which we could hardly make a track. We proceeded slowly at first because of the snow, and then detoured from the Hillary route to the left and on to the south spur. We arrived at some rock, and from here on things went a little better.

From 8.20 A.M. I was constantly in front. I believe that I have never in my whole life been in such excellent form.

. . . I can't describe to you what we thought. I only know that I had the feeling of being in the Zillertal [in the Tyrol], and that two words raced through my head whenever I felt unable to go on. You will probably no longer remember, but you once said to me when we were in the Penken hut (J. Cleare was with us): "You must go on, go on, go on!"

And these words were the only ones that went through my head. "Go on, go on, go on . . ."

I was about 20 meters [65 feet] above Reinhold, and perhaps that gave me the drive to show him that today I was better and stronger than he was. He noticed this too. I was still not certain in myself whether we would reach the summit!

At about 12 o'clock, I reached the South Summit, and there I knew for the first time that we would conquer the remaining meters up to the main summit. We were afraid only of the fearful wind which raged from the west over the summit ridge, and drove out a trail—several kilometers long—in the direction of Tibet.

Again I went on in advance. Compared with the ascent to the South Summit, it was a marvellous walk, because the ridge was completely swept off and we didn't sink in at all. We were very cautious of the gigantic snow cornices which project out in an easterly direction for fifty meters [160 feet] or more.

Reinhold filmed my ascent via the Hillary Step, and there, perhaps, I over exerted myself a little, because I climbed very quickly.

I had scarcely reached the top when I got cramp in my right hand, and this time I was really afraid. I had a vision of the Sherpa who had had a stroke in Camp III, and was completely paralyzed on his right side.

Reinhold was about 15 meters [50 feet] ahead. He had already reached the summit and was simply sitting there. I called out: "Film!" He did so, and when I was about 6 meters [20 feet] in front of him, I began to cry. I fell all over him; we blubbered like little children and took a few minutes to recover.

Our minds were completely blank. We simply automatically took a few film shots and photos of the summit. I had with me the Mayrhofen pennant, the ski school flag and a RAIKA emblem, but completely forgot about them. I no longer knew what I was thinking or feeling . . .

Again I felt the cramp in my hand, and now I knew that I

had to get down as quickly as possible to lower altitudes. I had no more strength for climbing. I sat down in the snow on the East Face, and just wanted to stay there forever.

Then I slid down the sixty-degree incline of the wall (on the Chinese side), down to an altitude of 8500 meters [27,886 feet]. It was crazy what I did, but it was mere instinct that guided me. During this slide down, only the Lord God was with me.

I kept on sliding down in the snow, and after a few seconds landed in the middle of an enormous snow shelf. I could no longer control myself, and lost my ax, goggles and crampons. I couldn't care less anymore, and simply thought: "Dying is so easy." A little later I lost consciousness for about ten minutes.

My "descent" had been watched by Eric Jones from the South Col. When the avalanche stopped, something dark lay in the middle of the snow shelf. He didn't know whether it was Reinhold or me. But he was certain that whoever it was must be dead.

Yesterday we arrived completely drained at the base camp. It will take days, perhaps a week, before we are our old selves again. We both have disorders of vision, but we will not go blind. I still do not know what happened to us, or how.

This ascent lies, without doubt, in the uttermost realm of human achievement. Least of all, altitude physicians will grasp the fact that we succeeded when nobody gave us any chance at all. The significance of the ascent will only become apparent in time.

When I think, however, of the sacrifices which this expedition has cost, it seems to me questionable whether the whole thing can be justified.

Peter Habeler after his return from the summit of Mount Everest. ▷ His face reflects his total exhaustion.

15

I HAD AGREED with Regina that during my Everest excursion she should go on a trip to America. I began to imagine to myself how it would be if I were to surprise her in Zurich on the twenty-seventh of May. On that day she was due to return.

But in between two interviews, Reinhold came toward me with a confidential-looking expression. He had heard that Regina was not in America at all, but that it was possible that she might be visiting us in the base camp.

The first part of this information was correct. She hadn't gone to America. This she had written in a letter to me in which, however, she mentioned nothing about a journey to Nepal. I was tense and excited, and although I wanted to get to the hospital in Khumde as quickly as possible, because of my painful ankle, I waited because I was afraid of missing her.

During the first days in the base camp, I was still rather confused. I seemed to see things from afar. Nothing seemed to affect me. I knew, it is true, that I had been on Everest; I knew it with my mind, but I hadn't really inwardly digested or assimilated this fact. Every night I repeated our ascent in my dreams. I suffered from terrible nightmares without knowing what they were about. It was as if I were going to suffocate, as if I were standing directly in front of the summit and couldn't inhale any more air into my lungs. Often I sat up bathed in sweat, and for minutes on end I didn't know where I was. I simply couldn't grasp that I was among people again and in safety.

A few times it seemed to me that my tent was full of insects. I shot up as if I had been stung by a tarantula and searched the whole tent for insects, which were naturally not there. On a couple of occasions I thought that everything was full of worms. Choked with disgust, I turned the tent inside out, until I finally became aware of where I was. Since then I haven't had any more dreams about worms and insects, but these dreams of suffocation still plague me. At such times I am saturated with sweat, and sometimes it happens that I don't even recognize my own wife when she wakes me.

After our adventure on the Hidden Peak in 1975, I had lapses of memory. During the descent I went through areas that seemed to me to be completely strange. And now, after Everest, it sometimes happens that at first sight I fail to recognize people who have been familiar to me for years.

"That will pass," the Bull consoled us. "Naturally some of your brain cells have been destroyed, particularly those that are connected with your memory of places and people. These cells can't be regenerated anymore, but other cells that have previously been unused, will take over their function."

My ankle was still causing me a lot of pain. I tried different ointments, but none of them was very successful.

A short time before, Jim, a New Zealand doctor, had come up to us from the Sherpa hospital in Khumde. I had placed my tent at his disposal, and he had invited me to stay with him should I, as was already planned anyway, leave the camp earlier. Now I decided to take advantage of this offer, in spite of the tempting prospect that Regina might visit me. I hoped to meet her on the way, if indeed she really should be coming up. There was only one spot where we could miss each other, that is on the serpentine track between Phakding and Namche Bazar. But she had to pass through Khumde in any case.

The two television reporters of the British HTV television company had already left us, while the two *Stern* magazine journalists were waiting for their helicopter to return, which had transported out an injured Sherpa. On the day of our return this Sherpa had fallen into a deep crevasse in the Khumbu Glacier, and had suffered serious injuries—in addition to a few bone fractures, an open skull fracture as well. He had to be taken to the Khumde Hospital as quickly as possible. But strangely enough, it was very difficult to move him at first from the site of the accident. The Sherpas seemed unwilling to help him, why we didn't know. It was perhaps connected with their mentality, which is basically incomprehensible to us, and will remain so. In any case, the *sahibs* had to step in and get the victim carefully, in a rescue sack, down to the valley to where the base camp lay.

On May 16, at one o'clock in the afternoon, I left the

base camp with a Sherpa, hobbled in one go, supported on a ski pole, down to Periche without turning round even once to look back at Everest. The next day I reached Khumde and went immediately to my friend Jim.

And here a tremendous surprise awaited me. Sir Edmund Hillary was there, the first conqueror of Everest. Hillary has devoted his whole life to the service of the Sherpas. He has collected donations from all over the world, and founded a whole series of schools and hospitals for the natives in Nepal, among them the hospital in Khumde where he had just arrived on an inspection tour.

Hillary congratulated me heartily on our success. "I have always believed," he said, "that one day the mountain would be conquered without oxygen. I am proud to be able to shake your hand."

It was a great moment for me. And now for the first time, as this dazzling hero of my childhood and youth shook my hand, I became aware of the importance of what we had actually achieved. We had written a new chapter in the history of alpine climbing. From now on, many mountaineers would be guided by our example, just as I had emulated Sir Edmund Hillary.

I stayed for a couple of days in the friendly hospital, always hoping to meet Regina, but she didn't show up. Instead, Reinhold appeared. He, too, had left the base camp earlier than was originally planned, and in the evening the four of us sat down together: Hillary, his brother, Reinhold and myself. Hillary told us about his numerous expeditions. There was one story that gave me much food for thought.

A few years ago he had tried to climb the 27,824-

foot-high Makālu, a neighboring mountain of Everest, without oxygen equipment. Hillary, too, had over the years become convinced that for mountaineering to remain a true sport, all too-technical aids should not be used. Like us, he had come to the conclusion that these highly technical expeditions had virtually nothing whatever to do with sport anymore. Yet he almost paid with his life for the attempt on the Makālu. He came down with a cerebral edema, and on the way back he also contracted an inflamation of the lung, which was a consequence of mountain sickness. Only rapid transportation down by helicopter saved his life, literally at the last minute.

Our days in the Himalayas were coming to an end. Regina had not arrived and I was becoming more and more anxious to return home. I wanted to see my wife and child again. We left Khumde by helicopter in the direction of Katmandu. As on the flight out, Bull was with us again, proud that he too achieved the victory over the summit. I was still confused, and still not fully in possession of my senses. Not yet completely my old self. I had difficulty in adapting myself again to reality.

From Katmandu we flew on, via Kuwait, to Frankfurt. From there we went back to Munich, to the starting point of our whole expedition. We were five hours late, and were doubtful as to whether anybody could be waiting for us at Munich. But when our plane came to a halt, I saw on the edge of the airport our dear old Mayrhofen band in their gray uniform jackets. They had loyally waited for us. I couldn't see Regina among them, but I

Homecoming reception in Munich.

hadn't really expected her. She hates standing in the limelight and, where possible, avoids appearing at official occasions.

And then, suddenly, she was standing before me. The airport administration had allowed her, alone, to pass. She embraced me and cried again, just as she had cried on my departure. I patted her and tried to calm her.

Reinhold Messner (left) and Peter Habeler (right) at Munich Airport on May 22, 1978.

When all the passengers had left the plane, we went to the gangway and stepped out into the bright sunlight. The band was playing, and Ernst Spiess was there and wiped his eyes. Full of emotion we embraced each other.

In the airport building an enormous delegation of

photographers and reporters were waiting for us. Strobe lights flared and we were showered with questions.

When the hullaballoo was finally over late in the evening, Regina and I were alone at last. I was glad to be going home, I was looking forward to the trip home in our car, and of course to seeing my son. Yet when I sat behind the steering wheel and prepared to start the car, I noticed that I was much too excited to drive, so I said to my wife: "You drive, Regina." She only smiled and didn't say a word. She understood my feelings.

Just two hours later we arrived in Mayrhofen.

It was the twenty-second of May 1978. I was home again.

APPENDIX

EVEREST WITHOUT OXYGEN:
THE MEDICAL FUNDAMENTALS
by Dr. Oswald Ölz

Physiological fundamentals:
oxygen starvation (anoxia) and acclimatization to it

The life-preserving oxygen blanket of our planet becomes more rarefied with increasing altitude; the oxygen density of the atmosphere (the oxygen partial pressure) at an altitude of 18,000 feet is only half the value of that at sea level; at 29,028 feet on the summit of Mount Everest it is only 32 percent.

This physical fact is the cause of the fundamental problem of mountaineering at high altitudes: the oxygen in the air is, with increasing altitude, less concentrated, consequently under lower pressure than in the lowlands, and the supply of essential gas to the body tissues is impaired.

This supply is made possible by the gradual oxygen pressure drop that exists along the oxygen supply chain of the organism. In other words, the oxygen concentration decreases constantly on its passage from the air outside to inhaled air in the pulmonary air cells (alveoli), then to arterial blood and finally to the tissue being supplied. In the atmosphere and in the alveoli, oxygen exists as free gas. In the blood it is for the greater part bound chemically to the hemoglobin, a transport pigment in the red blood corpuscles. In addition, a small part is dissolved in the blood plasma.

If the partial pressure of oxygen decreases with altitude, the oxygen pressure gradient levels off between alveolar air and arterial blood, and the hemoglobin is no longer completely charged or "saturated" with oxygen. On the summit of Mount Everest, the arterial oxygenation is only about 42 percent of the value at sea level. The resulting reduced oxygen evolution from the arterial blood to the tissues leads to tissue oxygen starvation, to hypoxia. This hypoxia is exclusively a result of the lowered oxygen partial pressure in the air; the simultaneous decrease of air pressure has no significance.

The organism has at its disposal a series of mechanisms in order to increase the oxygen capacity in the event of a lower oxygen content in the air, and thereby compensate to a certain extent for the lack of oxygen. The adaptation to altitude is made possible in this way. As a first reaction, the respiration is deepened and accelerated, whereby more oxygen is drawn into the lungs. Besides the desired increased intake of oxygen, this also has unfavorable results: the intensified respiration (hyperventilation) leads to the increased exhalation of carbon dioxide, and with it to a falling off of the acid content of the blood (respiratory alkalosis). The binding of the oxygen to the hemoglobin is thereby increased (left displacement of the oxygen dissociation curve), and the oxygen can only be discharged with difficulty from the arterial blood to the tissues.

During a longer stay at altitude, the alkalosis is corrected by increased secretion of bicarbonate in the kidney, whereby the oxygen dissociation is normalized again. Further quickly operative adaptation mechanisms are an increased circulation of blood in the lungs, which likewise furthers the oxygen absorption, as well as an intensification of the heart frequency and the blood volume assisted per heart action.

More arterial blood rich in oxygen thus travels in the time unit from the lung to the tissues. The tissue hypoxia stimulates the bone marrow to increased production of red blood corpuscles. The number of these corpuscles increases during a three- to four-week stay at an altitude of 13,000 feet by 20 to 25 percent (altitude polyglobulism). The hemoglobin content of the newly formed cells is increased. By means of both measures, the oxygen transport capacity of the blood is intensified.

The binding of the oxygen to the hemoglobin is reduced with the European mountaineer after a longer stay at altitude; thereby the evolution of oxygen to the tissues is facilitated (right displacement of the oxygen dissociation curve).

The biochemical basis of this is a rise in the diglycerophosphate content in the red corpuscles, which facilitates the oxygen discharge. Interestingly, this rise cannot be ascertained in the case of the Sherpas. Thus the red blood cells of the Sherpas bind oxygen more strongly than those of Europeans. The heightened binding capacity produces a more effective extraction of oxygen from the atmosphere into the blood. This apparent advantage would, however, be more than lost, because of a simultaneous reduction of the oxygen evolution to the tissues. The tissues would, in spite of a relatively high oxygen content, starve in the arterial blood.

With the Sherpas an additional, not yet investigated, mechanism seems to exist that nevertheless makes possible an easier discharge of oxygen to the tissues. This phenomenon has been interpreted as the result of a genetically conditioned adaptation. The Sherpas have lived for many thousands of years at altitudes over 9000 to 13,000 feet, which, through a change in the genotype and the pressure of selection, led to an unique adaptation to the low oxygen content of their environment. This biochemical mechanism certainly explains to some extent the extraordinary fitness of the Sherpas in high altitudes. At present, among further known changes in the organism, which enable an improved supply of oxygen, are an increase of the small blood vessels (capillaries) and with it a heightened circulation of blood in the muscular system.

Pathophysiology:
mountain sickness and high-altitude deterioration.

With too rapid an ascent to higher altitudes, the described adaptation mechanisms, which to a degree of 80 percent develop in ten to fourteen days, and of 95 percent in four to six weeks, are no longer sufficient to prevent severe hypoxia. As a direct and indirect consequence of hypoxia, the symptom complex of acute mountain sickness develops. With milder forms the patient suffers from headaches, loss of appetite, nausea and vomiting. Sleep is disturbed and every form of activity becomes an exertion. One's mental capacity is reduced.

Severe consequences of oxygen starvation include pulmonary edema, a concentration of water in the pulmonary vesicles, which makes breathing more and more impossible, as well as cerebral edema, an abnormal turgor of the brain due to the increased water content of the brain cells. All of this leads to nervous disorders and finally to unconsciousness. Both states are very serious, and lead rapidly to death if the patient is not immediately transported to lower altitudes and provided with oxygen and certain medicaments. By means of a systematic examination of members of expeditions to altitudes of 26,000 feet or more, a further potentially serious disorder brought on by altitude has been discovered during the past few years.

By means of the ophthalmoscope, small- to medium-sized hemorrhages can be identified in the back of the eye, the retina, of 30 to 40 percent of those mountaineers who stayed for longer periods at an altitude of over 19,000 feet. Mostly, the affected person notices nothing except for probable headaches. As long as the sources of the hemorrhage remain small, visual faculties are not impaired; one can, however, assume with certainty that in the case of the presence of retinal hemorrhages, similar hemorrhages will also appear in the brain. This can result in general changes in the brain functions and consequent fatigue, headaches, apathy and a slowing down, as well as special localized manifestations, such as uncertainty in walking and other disorders of movement.

Damage to the brain functions due to altitude is further possible through clots (thromboses) in the arteries supplying the brain or in the draining veins, whereby symptoms akin to a stroke can appear. The development of such thromboses is encouraged by changes in the blood-flow properties—hyperviscosity. This hyperviscosity is a result of the increase of the red blood cells, and is decisively aggravated if the alpine climber can no longer meet his enormous need for water at altitude—above 23,000 feet four to seven quarts every twenty-four hours —so that the organism, as it were, dries up.

The British mountaineers of the first Everest expeditions of 1921 and 1922 first observed a phenomenon for which they coined the term "High Altitude Deterioration." This is to be distinguished from acute mountain sickness and is exclusively the result of chronic oxygen starvation. It sets in even with fully trained and adapted climbers at altitudes of over 17,000 feet and signifies a constant deterioration of one's mental and physical condition. Genuine adaptation, and with it lasting survival, is not possible for human beings at altitudes much above 17,000 feet. Consequently, a genuine recuperation is only possible below this critical altitude. The highest human settlement, Aconquija in the Andes, lies at 16,400 feet. All attempts to settle higher have failed. The chronic lack of oxygen causes loss of appetite, a reduced intake of food, and thereby a dissolution of body protein and loss of weight.

The level of endurance and performance declines all the time. Naturally, the extent and the speed of high-altitude deterioration depends on the altitude, the length of time spent at that altitude and the individual constitution. While the well-adapted climber can survive and function adequately for months at 19,000 feet, at 26,000 feet this is possible only for days, if no artificial oxygen is used.

Hemodilution

An essential mechanism of adaptation to altitude is the increased formation of red blood cells in the bone marrow. In this way the oxygen transport capacity is increased. With optimal adaptation, the red blood cells in the peripheral blood rise by 20 to 25 percent of the initial value, the hematocrit, that is the percentage of red blood cells in the total bloodstream, is increased from 40 to 45 percent in the lowlands to 50 to 60 percent.

Higher values are only found if the climber has insufficiently met his need for liquid. This happens often, since, as already mentioned, this need over 23,000 feet is enormous (four to seven quarts every twenty-four hours), and at this altitude it is often wearisome and technically difficult to produce and drink so much liquid. With corresponding motivation and instruction, however, the liquid amount, even in an ascent of Mount Everest, can be controlled; the hematocrit values of our nine Everest climbers amounted to, on average, up to 55 percent 48 hours after reaching the summit. Messner and Habeler, who certainly were subjected to the hardest conditions, showed values of 58 and 54 percent respectively. The danger of a lack of fluid, which is indicated by hematocrit values of over 60 percent, lies in blood coagulation, the hyperviscosity syndrome. This results in deficient blood circulation through the tissues, and a consequent danger of frostbite, as well as a tendency to thromboses and hemorrhages, which are most deadly if localized in the brain.

Hemodilution, a process whereby before the ascent to the summit the hematocrit is lowered by means of a bloodletting of about 500 milliliters of blood, was recently tested as a preventative measure and recommended. The loss of blood volume is covered by infusion of blood plasma replacement. Through the reduction of hematocrit thus achieved, the flow qualities of the blood are improved. From the fact that ten out of thirteen members of the German Lhotse expedition in 1976 reached the summit after this treatment, it was concluded that an improvement of tissue blood circulation was attained, the danger of complications due to altitude lessened, and the drop in performance checked.

The idea that underlies hemodilution is interesting, but the hitherto published results do not allow for such conclusions. The experiments were carried out without any comparable monitoring group. Scientifically tenable conclusions cannot be drawn from the results. The very accomplished German Lhotse climbers, who also possessed excellent oxygen equipment, would very probably have been successful even without hemodilution. There is also the possibility that bloodletting has negative effects.

It must be remembered that the hematocrit increase conditioned by altitude is a physiologically significant adaptation mechanism, through which the supply of oxygen is improved. Further, this increase is exactly controlled by the organism and kept within sensible limits. A reduction of the hematocrit lessens the oxygen transport capacity of the blood. A hemodilution experiment carried out on the occasion of our expedition (reduction of the hematocrit from 61 to 53 percent) led to a drastic deterioration, lasting many days, in the previously excellent state of health of the person experimented on, in which, besides general weakness, symptoms of an incipient pulmonary edema arose.

After this, no further experiments of this type were carried out. The fact that nine out of ten climbers who undertook the assault on the summit in fact reached the summit without any damage to their health, as well as the fact that Everest was climbed by Messner and Habeler without using oxygen equipment, illustrate that mountaineering at great altitude can be free of complications, even without hemodilution. As long as the value of hemodilution is only postulated on the basis of anecdotal observations, and not proven in exact and incontestable experiments, this procedure remains an experimental one, and must be rejected as routine treatment owing to its potential harmfulness.

Possibilities and chances
of climbing without use of breathing apparatus

The prospects of success, and consequences of a climbing attempt without oxygen equipment, were vehemently discussed in wide circles before Messner and Habeler's march on the summit. Most of the experts and many climbers categorically declared the whole undertaking was impossible. These views were not based on physiological facts, but on personal opinions and prejudices. The old dogma: "Over 23,000 feet, survival without oxygen is impossible" is false; there is no rational physiological reason why for suitable, adapted individuals, short-term survival and functioning up to 29,500 feet altitude should be impossible.

All that is unclear is what physical and mental performance can be expected under these circumstances. The general opinion that Everest can only be conquered with oxygen apparatus first developed in the 1930s. The great British mountaineer Mallory, who was lost in 1924 at over 27,000 feet on the North Face of Everest, was convinced that Everest could be climbed without oxygen. Sir Edmund Hillary, too, the first conqueror of Everest, wrote in 1961: "Even the summit of Everest is not beyond the capacity of an unassisted man." Though at the same time he warned: "But the risks are enormous."

Fundamentals of climbing without use of oxygen equipment

The risks of an Everest ascent without oxygen equipment only differ in degree from the general risks of high-altitude climbing. Increasing reduction of bodily and mental performance can make the ascent impossible. The danger of frostbite is great, and eventually thromboses, hemorrhages, pulmonary and cerebral edema can arise.

The possibility that Messner and Habeler would, in the event of their success, return with severe brain damage, even as idiots, was frequently mentioned. The danger was, however, small. Lack of oxygen does indeed lead to diffuse and acute brain damage, with the resulting death of numerous brain cells. Neighboring, previously unused cells can, however, take over their function. Thus, for example, Messner's powers of memory after his suffering on the Nānga Parbat in 1970 were impaired for several weeks, only to recover completely. The history of alpine climbing shows further that no climber of twenty-six thousanders has returned from the summit mentally defective. Many of these men have later pursued extremely successful careers.

The basic fundamentals for the success of the two Tyrolean climbers are their exceptional physical and mental qualities, the use of a special technique, which is based on the experiences of other climbers, as well as, finally, the use of modern, lightweight equipment. The build of both men is thin and sinewy, almost ascetic. Clinical tests reveal nothing unusual apart from a slow relaxed pulse. We do not know if the climbers, particularly adept at high altitudes, possibly possess not yet identified or defined mechanisms, which depart biochemically from the norm, and which enable them to adapt better to lack of oxygen, as seems to be inborn in the Sherpas.

The outcome of the Everest experiment was decisively influenced by the motivation, toughness and intelligence as well as, in particular, the readiness and ability to bear pain and suffering. By means of all these factors it will become possible to push back the frontiers of endurance and, for example, to intensify the demands on the tortured muscular system over and above the barrier controlled by the nervous system. Through the tactics applied by Messner and Habeler already in the ascent of Hidden Peak, and now again on Everest, that is, to ascend from the base camp to the summit and return immediately, within a few days, the time spent above 24,000 feet was reduced to the minimum possible. This again reduced the extent of high-altitude deterioration to the barest minimum, and thereby saved up reserves for the success of an undertaking that seemed to most people up to May 8, 1978, hopeless, and which then finally demonstrated the elegance of "mountaineering without tricks."